An Historical Description of the Zetland Islands. Repr

Thomas Gifford

HISTORICAL DESCRIPTION

OF THE

ZETLAND ISLANDS

IN THE YEAR 1733.

WORKS RELATIVE TO

ORKNEY AND SHETLAND

ON SALE AT THE

𝕎ell-known Antiquarian and Historical Book-Shop

OF

THOMAS GEORGE STEVENSON,

22 Frederick Street, Edinburgh.

I.—RENTALL OF THE PROVOSTRIE OF ORKNEY, A.D. M.D.LXXXIV. Edited by J. A. Maconochie, *Sheriff of Orkney.* 4to,—"NOT PRINTED FOR SALE,"—*stitched.* 2s. 6d.   1840

II.—MACKENZIE'S (James, *Writer, Kirkwall*) General Grievances and Oppression of the Isles of ORKNAY and SHETLAND, with an Appendix of Documents, 1750. *New Edition,* with a Memoir of the Author, and Illustrative Notes by GROAT and CHEYNE. Sm. 8vo, *boards.* 3s.
                                                                    1836

> *⁎* "This highly interesting work has special reference to the LAWSUIT (which occurred about the middle of the last century), raised at the instance of several of the Orkney heritors against the Earl of Morton, and which is commonly called 'THE PUNDLAR PROCESS.'"
>
> ☞ "THE REAL WRITER of this work,—of which only two parts appeared,—was JAMES FEA, Surgeon, on whose abilities it reflects great credit. It was originally printed for private circulation, and the impression limited to fifty copies."

III.—MONTEITH (Robert, *of Eglisha and Gairsa*), THE DESCRIPTION OF THE ISLES OF ORKNAY AND ZETLAND, in the year 1633. *Reprinted from the Edition of 1711,* published under the Superintendence of SIR ROBERT SIBBALD. 8vo, *with two beautiful facsimiles of the exceedingly rare maps, boards.* 7s. 6d.   1845

> *⁎* "ONLY ONE HUNDRED AND FIFTY-FIVE COPIES PRINTED."

IV.—GIFFORD'S (Thomas, *of Busta*) HISTORICAL DESCRIPTION OF THE ZETLAND ISLANDS in the year 1733. With an Appendix of Historical Documents. *Reprinted from the Original Edition* published in 1786 under the superintendence of JOHN NICHOLS, London. With an Introductory Notice. 8vo, *map, boards.* 10s. 6d.   1879

> ☞ "Displays a degree of research that would do credit to the topography of any province. IT IS AN EXCELLENT WORK."
>
> *⁎* "GIFFORD'S position as a native of Shetland, with a large property, and extensive connections as a merchant, gave him exceptional opportunities for understanding the circumstances of the country in his own day, and entitle his 'Historical Description' to be received as an authority on all matters coming within the range of his observation. IT IS EXTREMELY INTERESTING AND VALUABLE TO THE STUDENT OF THIS PORTION OF NORTHERN HISTORY."
>
> ☞ "IMPRESSION LIMITED TO ONE HUNDRED COPIES."

HISTORICAL DESCRIPTION

OF THE

ZETLAND ISLANDS

IN THE YEAR 1733.

𝕎ith an 𝔄ppendix of 𝔦llustrative 𝔇ocuments.

BY

THOMAS GIFFORD, OF BUSTA,

STUART AND JUSTICIAR-DEPUTE OF ZETLAND.

Reprinted from the Original Edition published in 1786 under the
superintendence of

JOHN NICHOLS, LONDON.

EDINBURGH:

THOMAS GEORGE STEVENSON,

22 FREDERICK STREET.

M.DCCC.LXXIX.

Gough Adds Islands
8vo 86.

IMPRESSION.

ONE HUNDRED COPIES FOR SUBSCRIBERS.

R. SYME AND SON, PRINTERS, EDINBURGH

Contents.

INTRODUCTORY NOTICE.

IN that very interesting and highly valuable, but now much neglected, bibliographical work, entitled "BRITISH TOPOGRAPHY; or, An Historical Account of what has been done for illustrating the TOPOGRAPHICAL ANTIQUITIES of GREAT BRITAIN and IRELAND, by RICHARD GOUGH," 2 vols. 4to, 1780,* there is to be found, under the head of "Scottish Topography," Descriptive Notices of the various Manuscripts, Printed Books, Charts, Maps, and Views, &c., pertaining to the "ISLANDS ON THE COASTS OF SCOTLAND." It was in that work that the FIRST NOTICE descriptive of the ORIGINAL MANUSCRIPT of Gifford's "Description of Zetland" appeared. It is as follows:—" Thomas Gifford of Busta, Esq., in the year 1733 wrote a ' Description of Zetland,' consisting of seven chapters : 1. contains a geographical description of the isles of Zetland, their extent and divisions into parishes. 2. Of the first inhabitants of Zetland and its name. 3. A description of the air, soil, and product, of Zetland. 4. Of the manners, language, and religion. 5. Of the government of Zetland, ancient and modern. 6. Of the ancient and modern way of transmitting property in Zetland. 7. Of the several denominations of the crown rents of Zetland, their original and how paid. With an Appendix, containing Alexander

* RICHARD GOUGH.—This illustrious Antiquary and Topographer,—"The Camden of the eighteenth century,"—was born 21st October 1735 and died 20th February 1809. All of his topographical collections, together with all his books relating to Saxon and Northern Literature, maps, and engravings, &c., &c., were left to the Bodleian Library, his miscellaneous library being sold by auction in 1810. Mr. John Nichols was the executor. A very full memoir of him is to be found in "Nichols' Literary Anecdotes of the Eighteenth Century." 1812-1815. 9 vols., 8vo.

Douglas,

Douglas of Spynie, chamberlain of the earldom of Orkney and lordship of Zetland, his charter granted to the heritors of Zetland upon their udell lands, dated 1664: also copy of his feu charter granted to the feuers of the crown land in Zetland, dated same year; and queen Anne's gift of the islands of Orkney and Zetland to the right hon. the earl of Morton, dated at Kensington 1st February 1707-8; superscribed by her majesty, and subscribed by Queensberry, Seafield, Montrose, Galloway, Forfar, F. Montgomery, Mar, Loudon, Weems, Northesk, Leven, Cromarty, J. Murray, Archibald Douglas, and John Erskine: then follows an abridgement of the country Acts; ferry freight to and from the different islands (in Scots money), with the country act about parochial schools 14th November 1724; and compend of the country acts for directing the *rancelmen,* and society for regulating of servants and reformation of manners, with their instructions; concluding with a scheme for regulating the German and Danish current money passing here. M.S. in 173 pages 4to, to which is prefixed a drawing of the mainland, with the islands belonging thereto. Mr. Paton has seen the copy, which was presented to the earl of Morton, when President of the Royal Society [London]. It is written and signed by Mr. Gifford, and still remains in the noble family library; but copies were given by the author to others, whereof Mr. Paton has a transcript." *

---

* GEORGE PATON (clerk in the Custom House, Edinburgh), was the son of John Paton, a much esteemed bookseller in the Parliament Square. For a long series of years he devoted himself to the study of Scotish Antiquities. A keen Bibliographer and Antiquary, he was well-known to almost all the literary characters of his own country, and to many English Antiquarians and men of letters. The chief aim of his ambition seemed to be the acquisition of such memorials of antiquity as might tend to elucidate the Literature, History, and Topography of his native country. Among the many who experienced his friendly aid, none has more gratefully expressed it than Mr. Gough, who speaks of him in the preface to the "British Topography" as "I should be wanting in gratitude were I not to express my particular obligations to my very ingenious and communicative friend, Mr. George Paton, of Edinburgh, who has spared no trouble or expense to enlarge the Article of Scottish Topography."

Although Mr. Paton assisted in the publication of various works, it is not believed that he ever produced anything of his own. He died upon the 6th

During

During the years 1780-1794 there was printed a series of extremely valuable "TOPOGRAPHICAL TRACTS," under the title of "BIBLIOTHECA TOPOGRAPHICA BRITANNICA," edited and published by JOHN NICHOLS, London. In this work Gifford's "Historical Description of Zetland" was *first printed*, with an explanatory preface by the editor. *

In the PREFACE (p. vi.) mention is made of "Captain JOHN SMITH" having, when on his way to Shetland, "came to anchor before Leith in Scotland, May 13, 1633, where, going on shore, and thence to Edinburgh, he delivered his letters to Mr. WILLIAM DICK, who was at that time Governor of the Island of Shetland, and did receive the revenue of

March 1807, at the age of 87 years, greatly regretted by those who had the pleasure of being acquainted with him. His books, probably the most curious and valuable collection of the kind ever exposed to sale in this country, were sold by auction in the year 1809, (the sale commencing on the 27th February and ending the 25th March thereafter); and his manuscripts, prints, coins, &c., were subsequently disposed of in a similar manner in 1811. (The sale commenced on the 2d and terminated on the 12th of December).

Of the "PATON COLLECTION OF LETTERS," preserved in the Library of the Faculty of Advocates, Edinburgh, two volumes have been published, viz.:— I. "Letters from Joseph Ritson to George Paton, 1792–1795." Sm. 8vo. (John Stevenson, Edinburgh, 1829.) II. "Letters from Thomas Percy, D.D., afterwards Bishop of Dromore, John Callander, of Craigforth, David Herd, and others, to George Paton, 1768–1789." Sm. 8vo. (John Stevenson, Edinburgh, 1830.) These volumes, not generally known, are enriched with very interesting and curious notes, highly illustrative of various points in the literary history of Scotland during the latter part of the last century, by JAMES MAIDMENT, Advocate, Edinburgh.

The entire "GOUGH AND PATON" Correspondence (comprising a period from the year 1771 to 1804), are also preserved in the Advocates' Library, Edinburgh. They are infinitely more interesting in every respect, full of important literary and topographical information. In 1842 proposals were issued for the publication of these letters by subscription, under the editorship of W. B. D. D. TURNBULL, Advocate. But as the publication would have been attended with considerable risk, it was judged expedient, before going to press, to have at least one hundred subscribers, the expense attendant on such an undertaking absolutely requiring patronage to that extent. As the number of patrons did not come up to the expectations of the editor and publisher, the idea was abandoned.

* JOHN NICHOLS, Printer.—This amiable and industrious man was either author or editor of upwards of sixty different works. A memoir of him by Alexander Chalmers, with a list of his publications, appeared in the "Gentleman's Magazine" for December 1826, of which valuable periodical he was editor and proprietor for many years.

these

these islands." This person was the grandson of ALEXANDER DICK of Braid, near Edinburgh, the Provost of the Cathedral Church of Orkney. He, adopting from his youth the profession of commerce, became one of the most eminent bankers in Scotland, and acquired considerable wealth, which appears by his advancing to King James VI. six thousand pounds sterling, to defray the household expenses when his majesty held a parliament in Scotland in 1618. In 1628 he farmed the customs on Wine, at six thousand and two hundred and twenty-two pounds sterling, and the Crown Rents in Orkney at three thousand pounds sterling per annum, and afterwards the Excise. He was elected Lord Provost of Edinburgh in 1638 and in 1639, and after receiving the honour of knighthood in 1646, was created a baronet of Nova Scotia. Sir William suffered severely during the Commonwealth, being fined by the Parliamentarians as a malignant, in no less a sum than sixty-four thousand nine hundred and thirty-four pounds, so that from a state of considerable opulence he was reduced with his family to very indigent circumstances. He repaired in consequence to London to demand repayment of a very large sum of money which he had previously advanced upon government security, and was there thrown into prison by Cromwell, and died at Westminster, 19th December 1655.

In addition to the information contained in the preface by JOHN NICHOLS as to THOMAS GIFFORD of Busta, author of the "Historical Description of the Zetland Islands, printed in 1786," I am enabled to give the following new particulars as to him and his family connections.

In the "Register of Ministers, Exhorters, and Readers, and of their Stipends, after the period of the Reformation," printed for the "Maitland Club, Glasgow," 4to, 1830, it is recorded that "John Giffart, reidar in North Mavin, 1567," had "the thryd of the vicarage extending to xx *li.*" (£1, 13s. 4d.), and that in 1576, "Johnne Giffert, minister, had for serving St. Colmis Kirk, Croce Kirk, and Olaberry in North Mavin, his stipend xx *li.*, and for payment thairof, the haill thrid of his awin vicarage of North Mawing, xx *li.*

xx *li. eque,* and to uphald ane reidare, and to have thairfoir
ane barrell butter furth of the Bishopis bothis of the said
Parochine." In Scott's " *Fasti Ecclesiæ Scoticanæ,*" 1871,
4to, it is stated that " He died prior to 10th July 1577.
He is said to have become a Protestant that he might marry
a lady at Aberdeen. From him are descended the Giffords
of Busta."

On the 28th January 1728, William Gifford, son of
John Gifford of Busta, was licensed by the Presbytery of
Linlithgow, called in September following, and ordained
Minister of the parish of North Maving, at Olaberry, 6th
March 1729. He died 27th March 1767, and Bess Leslie,
his widow, died 11th August 1776.

THOMAS GIFFORD, the author of the " Historical Description written in the year 1733," was proprietor of the
estate of Busta in Shetland, to which he succeeded on the
death of his father, John Gifford.

Thomas Gifford was a Whig, attached to the Hanoverian
succession, while the principal Shetlanders were mostly
Tories and Jacobites. Through his political relations in this
way he received from the Earl of Morton the appointment of
" Stuart and Justiciar Depute of Zetland," and attained to
much local influence in the troublous times of the Jacobite
risings in the last century ; while, as a successful merchant
and otherwise, he was enabled to consolidate his patrimo-
nial estate, with extensive additions, as the largest property
in Shetland. He died in 1760, and his wife Elizabeth
Mitchell, sister of Sir John Mitchell of Westshore, Bart.,
in 1769. Their remains were interred in the family tomb
at Olnafirth Church. They had a large family, all of
whom died in infancy, except four sons, John, Robert,
William, and Hay, and three daughters, Margaret, Chris-
tina, and Andrina. All the four sons were drowned, along
with their cousin and tutor, the Rev. John Fisken, by the
upsetting of a boat in Busta Voe, on the 14th May 1748.

Thomas Gifford having no surviving male issue, he
adopted, as his heir, Gideon Gifford, posthumous child of
his deceased eldest son John, by Miss Barbara Pitcairn, to
whom he had never been publicly married. Gideon, who

died

died in 1811, was succeeded by his son, the late Arthur Gifford of Busta, who died in 1856, and whose service as nearest and lawful heir in general to his great-grandfather, the author of the "Historical Description" was the subject of a protracted litigation at the instance of Arthur Gifford (son of Andrew Gifford of Ollaberry, who died in 1810), R.N., in Canada, claiming service (9th November 1832) as heir-at-law and heir of entail, on the ground of the alleged illegitimacy of Busta's father, Gideon Gifford. The service was obtained under an Advocation of Brieves tried at Edinburgh, on the 7th February 1833, before Lord Moncrieff and a professional jury, who, after a voluminous proof, returned a verdict for the defendant (Busta.)

The Pursuer (Ollaberry) after various proceedings in the Court of Session in reference to the effect of the decision in the Chancery Court (1833), and for permission to produce new and additional evidence (1835), which the court refused, on the motion of the Lord Justice-Clerk (Boyle), who remarked. "I do not think we can listen to the pursuer's demand in *hoc statu*, so long as he adheres to his first plea in law, (that he was not precluded from offering further evidence, by his having appeared in the process of competition.) There was here a competition of brieves, where both parties had full opportunities of leading proof. There was no allegation of informalities having occurred. The verdict was solemnly returned, and we cannot neglect it. But I reserve my opinion as to the competency of leading new evidence when the question is brought forward in a proper shape. If it should be allowed, it will be a nice question in what manner this additional evidence is to be let in." The pursuer thereafter (17th February 1837) raised a Process of Reduction of the verdict of the jury (1833), when the court "reviewing the whole evidence led before the inquest, found that the verdict could not be maintained." The pursuer on application was afterwards (16th July 1837) granted expenses.

Mr. Thomas Gifford's position as a native of Shetland, with a large property, and extensive connections as a merchant, gave him exceptional opportunities for understanding

ing the circumstances of the country in his own day, and entitle his " Historical Description " to be received as an authority on all matters coming within the range of his observation.   At the same time, his memory extended so near to the period of the transition from ancient laws and institutions in the islands to modern usages, that his descriptions of these, though perhaps not always strictly accurate, are yet extremely interesting and valuable to the student of this portion of northern history.

DR. SAMUEL HIBBERT, who appears to have made much use of " Gifford's Work," in the compiling of his " Description of the Shetland Islands," 1822, 4to, remarks (1.) that " Gifford's Memoir of Shetland, drawn up eighty years ago, displays a degree of research that would do credit to the Topography of any Province ;" and, (2.) " This is an excellent work; it was written in the year 1733, in conformity to the wish of the Earl of Morton, by whom he was appointed a steward-depute in the county ; but the fear of offending this nobleman by allusions to the conduct of his ancestors, led him to be very careful of entering with great particularity into the history of Udel Tenures.   It is indeed questionable if, after all, Earl Morton did not think that he had explained too much on the subject."

MR. ALEXANDER G. GROAT, Advocate, in his " Thoughts on Orkney and Zetland," 8vo, (privately printed), 1831, remarks, that " It is a singular fact, that most of those who have made researches into the antiquities of Orkney and Zetland, have not been natives of these islands; and it is still more singular, that comparatively little is known on the subject in the district.   We question whether nine-tenths of its best-informed inhabitants have ever even heard the names of one-half of the works that have been written about Orkney and Zetland."

The extreme rarity of the " Bibliotheca Topographica Britannica," and the consequent inaccessibility of Gifford's " Historical Description" separately, has induced me to undertake the reprinting of such a curious and highly instructive work.   The original printed edition contains some errors, especially in the form of place-names, in most

cases

cases obvious misprints, from erroneous reading of the manuscript. In the map of the Islands prefixed to it, and now re-produced in facsimile, the place-names are also carelessly rendered. Some of these errors have found their way into the text, but while desiring to adhere as closely as possible to the original, the more obvious misprints of the kind have been altered in the List of Inhabited Islands, Parishes, &c. (page 2). The impression printed has been limited to ONE HUNDRED COPIES, chiefly to gratify the wishes and supply the wants of collectors of such out-of-the-way rare and interesting historical and topographical relics.

In conclusion, I beg to return my best thanks to GILBERT GOUDIE, Esq. (one of the Translators of the " Orkneyinga Saga," 8vo, 1873) for kindness and information received during the course of this volume through the press.

EDINBURGH, 22 FREDERICK STREET,
July 1879.

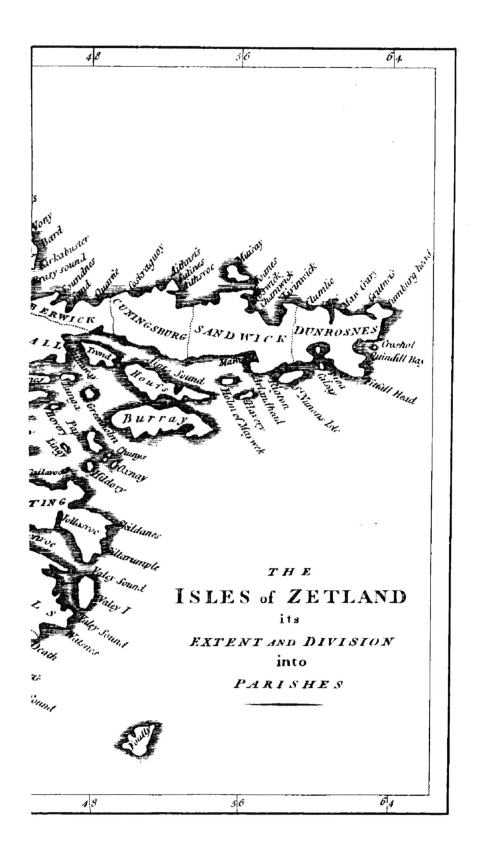

THE
ISLES of ZETLAND
its
EXTENT AND DIVISION
into
PARISHES

AN

HISTORICAL

DESCRIPTION

OF THE

ZETLAND ISLANDS.

By THOMAS GIFFORD, Esq.

LONDON:

PRINTED BY AND FOR J. NICHOLS,

PRINTER TO THE SOCIETY OF ANTIQUARIES.

MDCCLXXXVI.

CONTENTS.

PREFACE, with Additions.

TABLE OF CHAPTERS.

APPENDIX.

PREFACE.

THE description of ZETLAND here offered to the public was written by Thomas Gifford of Busta, esquire, 1733, in 173 pages 4to, to which was prefixed a drawing of the main land with the islands thereto belonging. The original MS. is in the hands of the author's family. A copy of it was presented to the Earl of Morton when president of the Royal Society, written and signed by Mr. Gifford, and still remains in the noble family library. Copies were given by the author to other persons; and a transcript of one of them falling into the hands of Mr. George Paton of Edinburgh,[1] was, with the spirit of liberal communication which so eminently marks his character, imparted to the editor of the Bibliotheca Topographica Britannica [1780-90, 8 vols. 4to.]

The first description we have in print of this island, or rather collection of thirty-three inhabited islands, seems to have been included in "England's Improvement revived, digested into six books, by captain John Smith, 1670,"[2] 4to. The first five books of this work treat of the improvements that might be made in planting and raising timber; and the sixth was printed first by itself, 1662. The author being apprentice to Mr. Matthew Cradock, of London, merchant, one of the society for the fishing trade of Great Britain, was sent to sea by the Earl of Pembroke, and his associates, for the discovery of the island of *Shetland*, the manner and way of trading, the profits and customs thereof, the settling a staple building of storehouses, viewing

1 British Topography, [by Gough], vol. II. p. 730.
2 This seems to be the same mentioned in the list prefixed to Gibson's Camden.

the

the ground on shore for landing and drying of nets, making and drying of fish, and building of blockhouses for the security of trade. He sailed from Gravesend April 27, 1633, was forced by foul weather into Harwich, and detained there till the 30th. The wind not favouring he anchored in Yarmouth Road, and there going on shore, learnt that the Hollanders' busses did drive at sea for herrings on that coast, and that from the Holmes before Yarmouth to Bookness [Buchanness] in Scotland, N.N.E. is 96 leagues, and from Bookness to the south end of Shetland, N. and by E. about 53 leagues. May 5, he sailed from Yarmouth, and by stress of wind was forced into Scarbrough, and there going on shore, was informed of the Hollanders' busses fishing on that coast, and that from Scarbrough northward toward Catness, in 45 fathom, or ·thereabouts, in that fair way are usually the first summer herrings caught. From Scarbrough he sailed and came to an anchor before Leith in Scotland, May 13, where going on shore, and from thence to Edinburgh, he delivered his letters to Mr. William Dicks, who was at that time governor of the island of Shetland, and did receive the revenue of those islands. Having received instructions and letters from Mr. Dicks to Mr. James Scot, who lived at the time in the north parts of the island of Shetland, and was agent or deputy to the said William Dicks, he sailed from Leith, and came to anchor at Casten in the island of Orkney, May 22. These islands he briefly describes, adding, that those of Faro lye from Shetland westerly, about 58 leagues.

The south part of Shetland lyeth about thirty leagues northward from the said island called *Maland*. He sailed from Casten and came to an anchor by Sundbroug-head, the south part of Shetland, June 3, and going ashore spake with the good man of *Quandale*, one of the chief of those parts, who with other of the inhabitants informed him of their manner of trading with the Hamburghers and others, and of the Hollanders fishing for herrings on that coast, and of their dogger boats that fish only for ling and cod. He next anchored in *Bracey* [Brassa] *Sound*, otherwise called *Broad Sound*, a very gallant harbour, where many

ships

ships may lie land-lockt for all winds. After informing himself of the trade and fisheries carried on there, he next visited *Evey Sound*, the northernmost sound in Shetland, June 12, and there going on shore continued about 11 or 12 months, and in that time travelled the greatest part of the island by sea and land.

" The land of Shetland lyeth N. and by E. and S. or S. and N. about 60 miles. But there are many islands belonging to Shetland. That which is most considerable are the sounds and harbours. On the west side of the southward point of Shetland is a good harbour and sound, called *St. Magnus*, and on the east side near *Sunbroughhead* is a fair sand-bay, where there is good anchorage in 10 or 12 fathom. To the northward of this last sound is another sound called *Hambrough haven*, which is a ladeplace for the Hamburghers and Scotch. About 9 or 10 leagues from the southward part of Shetland there is a channel that runneth through the land ; the south part of the land divided by the channel is called *Swanberg*, the other part so divided on the north part *Laxford*. Within the channel aforesaid are several sounds or harbours, but the best and chiefest sound in Shetland is *Brace Sound* or *Broad Sound*, as before-mentioned. Out of this sound the aforesaid channel doth run northward. On the north part of Swanbergh lieth the high hill of *Hangrix*, from which, about 9 leagues northward, lie some out rocks, called *the Stars*. To the northward of these is a very good harbour, called *Bloom Sound* ; north of this is another good haven, called *Hue Sound*, being the northern or north-east sound or haven belonging to the island called *Ounst*. There are other havens or sounds which lye through the land between and about that part of Shetland called *Laxford*, and the island called *Jello*. There are also other islands and sounds, which for brevity sake I forbear to mention.

" The merchants which trade with the inhabitants of Shetland are Hamburghers, Bremers, Luberghers, Scots, and English. The chief merchants of the islands are Scots, the meaner and inferior sorts are a mixt people of Danes and Scots. The islands of Shetland, as I have been informed

formed, were given to King James of blessed memory, by the king of Denmark, with queen Anne, in part of her dowry. The commodity of Shetland, which the merchants do for the most part trade with them is ling and cod, which they take with hooks and lines in small boats called *yawls*, about the beginning of Gravesend ocean. The ling they sell for three pence a pound, being a ling of the larger size, and called a *gild ling*; if smaller, we have two for one, or three for two, and so proportionable. The cod is sold for two pence the *gild cod*, and is measured as the ling. I bought of fisherman merchants of the island of Ounst, 11655 gild ling, and 834 gild cod, at three pence the gild ling, and two pence the gild cod, which ling and cod were taken by the said fisherman at several times in the small boats, and brought to my booth or place of abode every morning as they were caught. The said ling and cod being very good and merchantable, were salted on board the ship that landed me, and within seven weeks after my landing, I sent her for London with the said fish to the Earl of Pembroke. There are also other small fish, which the inhabitants do catch with angles, sitting in the rocks and in their small boats with hooks and lines in the soundings and between the islands; and these small fish are very considerable, for though they cannot spend them by reason of the multitude which they take, and have not industry to make use of them for transportation; yet the livers they preserve, and with the livers of the ling and cod make train oil; but if it were improved as taking them with nets, the train oil would amount to a considerable sum; and if this measure of trade were carried through the whole island, it would be a great encouragement to all merchants trading into those parts. Several other merchants in the island where I inhabited bought ling and cod of the fishermen, so that the quantity which I sent for England was not above the fifth part taken in that island, which with the whole quantity of fish bought by other merchants throughout the whole island of Shetland being added to them would amount to a very considerable sum, or quantity to the lading of many vessels, which might be

much

much more improved and increase trade, and thereby furnish the inhabitants with money and commodities.

In the island of Shetland were beeves and sheep, sold at a very reasonable rate. I bought for my own use in victualling the ship sent to London three oxen for three pounds; and at another time, four for five pounds, which were fat, and about the bigness of the smaller sort of cattle which we have in England. There were also fat sheep sold for two shillings, and two shillings and six-pence per sheep. There were also other creatures for food, as conies and fowl. The fuel or firing is peat and turf. There may be salt pans set up, and good salt made to serve all the fishing fleet. There are very good shores for landing and drying of nets, and making and drying of fish. There is no night in the north of Shetland part of two months in the year, as June and July.

In an island north of Ounst, being not inhabited, but stocked with wild cows and conies, I killed with my birding pieces ten couple of coneys in one night, from sun-set to sun-rise, and it was as light as a cloudy winter. I do not remember any frost or snow in Shetland; if any, it was not of long continuance. The coldest weather is by reason of great winds in the winter quarter, the wind blowing so violent, that no ship dare look on the north coast, so that the people of those islands have little communication with other nations in that quarter. I can speak by experience: being blown down flat to the ground by the violence of the wind, I was forced to creep on hands and knees to the next wall, and going by the wall, got into an house, or else must have stood by the wall till the violence of the wind were over. Sometimes it lasted half a day or more. There are several towns in Shetland so called, having about eight or ten houses together, where they plow and sow corn, as oats, which is their chiefest bread; and if my memory do not much deceive me, there was good barley growing in my time; but the land might be much improved if the inhabitants were industrious. They are like the idle Irish, not improving anything either by sea or land, spending that in winter which they get in summer, though their winter
might

might be very profitable to them, if they were laborious
and industrious as the Hollanders.

The goods and commodities that are vendible in Shetland
are hooks and lines for taking ling and cod, nets for taking
herrings, strong beer, biscuit, wheaten meal, salt, peas,
fruits of all sorts, strong water, Monmouth caps, and many
other particulars. The inhabitants of Ounst usually have a
bark that they trade with to Norway, where they may buy
timber for houses ready framed, deal boards, tar, ships,
barks and boats of all sorts, and other necessaries for their
use. With these small fishing boats, called yawls, they
will row into the main about two or three leagues, where
the banks are, on which they lay their hooks and lines for
ling and cod. In one of these boats, rowing with two men,
and sometimes four, according to the largeness of the boat,
they usually bring to shore every morning that they go to
sea about fifty or sixty ling and cod. There are many
barrels of herrings taken by the inhabitants with their
small boats in the Sound and at sea, not far from land,
which are the gleanings of the Hollanders busses, for the
busses driving at sea break the scull or shoal of herrings,
and then the herrings flee near the shore and through the
Sound, where these small boats with those nets they have
take them, but if they had better tackle and boats they
might take 500 barrels for one, which would much inrich
the island, and by increasing trade augment his majesty's
revenue."

Thus far Captain Smith.

The result of his observations was a plan for England
to fit out a fleet of busses for the fishing trade here, and
exclude all foreigners from fishing and trading in the
islands of Orkney and Shetland.

The next authentic account of these islands was given
by Mr. Thomas Preston, in two letters to Mr. Joseph
Ames, dated Jan. 31, 1743-4, printed in the Philosophical
Transactions, No. 473, p. 57, which, as it follows Mr. Gifford
very close in point of time, we shall give at large in the
Appendix.

A description of the islands of Orkney and Zetland was
advertised

advertised in the Edinburgh Evening Courant, of August 24, 1771, as preparing for the press, to give " an account of " their fisheries, commerce, manufactures, natural curiosi- " ties, antiquities, plants, minerals, state of agriculture, num- " ber of inhabitants, public buildings, &c. from the earliest " account of these islands to the present times." Such gen- tlemen as had anything to communicate concerning them, which is not mentioned by Wallace or Mackenzie, were de- sired to transmit their materials to A. Donaldson, bookseller in Edinburgh, or to William Coke, bookseller in Leith, who was then at Kirkwall in Orkney ; but of this design nothing further has transpired, and it seems rather to be laid aside.

" The description of the isles of Orknay and Zetland " with the mapps of them, done from the accurat observa- " tions of the most learned who lived in those isles," pub- lished by Sir Robert Sibbald, Ed. 1711. fol. seems to be taken from various accounts. Captain Smith is cited in it.[1] John Bruce, of Simbister, surveyed all the coast of Shet- land, and " made a large map of all the *Voes*, i.e. bays and sounds, and the entries to them, and marked the meaths in them, and showen where dangers are, and how they are to be avoided ; and resolved as soon as he goes home to take a more exact survey of all again, and to miss no bank, rock, nor shallow." This description is divided into twelve chapters,[2] in the last of which these islands are supposed to be the Thule mentioned by Tacitus, on which idea, in which Hector Bactus [Boethius] anticipated him, Sir Robert wrote a fuller dissertation, first printed at the end of Wallace's description of Orkney, 1693, 1700 ; and in bishop Gibson's first and succeeding editions of Camden's Britannia.

John Brand's "new description of Orkney, Zetland, Pight- " land-firth, and Caithness, Edinburgh, 1703," 8vo. professes " to give a particular view of the several isles thereto be-

---

1 [This work, which was written by Robert Monteith of Eglisha and Gairsa, 1633, was Reprinted in octavo, with facsimiles of the two rare Maps, by Thomas G. Stevenson, Edinburgh, 1845.]

2 Bishop Nicolson, in his Scottish Historical Library, p. 55, [London, 1702], gives a different enumeration of the chapters of this work, which would lead one to suspect he had seen a different work.

longing,

" longing, together with an account of what is most rare
" and remarkable therein." But as he was an itinerant
missionary preacher, he has inserted all the legendary
stories [1] so roundly believed by the common people, and
converted every uncommon fish into an evil spirit.[2] He
speaks highly of the civility and hospitality of the people,
and their attention to religion, where they had an opportunity of hearing sermons, but laments the want of schools,
particularly a good Latin one. His description of Zetland
takes up about 70 pages.

Among Macfarlane's MS. Collections now in the Advocates' Library at Edinburgh is a general geographical description of Zetland, by Mr. Hugh Leigh, minister of Brassie
and Buro.[3]

Mr. Wallace promised a full description of the western
islands, Shetland, and those in Edinburgh Frith, by his
father, with maps of the most considerable.[4]

Mr. Martin, at the end of his description of the western
isles of Scotland, 1697, 1703, and 1716, gives a short account of Schetland or Zetland ; but this is only an abridgement of Mr. Wallace's. Martin never was there ; and
Brand supplies many defects in Wallace ; yet both of them
are far from being full, accurate, or entertaining, says Mr.
Toland in his MS. notes on Martin's book. " I shall say
nothing here," continues he, " of those two clusters of
islands; but though I am persuaded *Iceland* to have been
the true *Thule* of the ancients, yet that seen by the Roman
fleet when it sailed round Britain in Vespasian's time was
HETLAND. The words of Tacitus are, *Dispecta est et*
Thule *quam hactenus nix et hiems abdebat.*[5] This passage
just follows his mention of the discovery of the Orcades,
so that nothing can be plainer, the ships having sailed between them."

From Brand and Wallace was compiled the account of Zetland in the "System of Geography," 1741,382; and the Tours
through Great Britain have drawn from the same source.

---

1 Spirit *Browney* appears to be as much the Genius of these islands as of
Cornwall, and had his share of every dairy, harvest, or brewery.
2 See p. 113–115.
3 Brit. Top. vol. II. p. 729.   4 Ib. 730.   5 Vit. Agr.

The

The " Voyages to Shetland, the Orkneys, and Western Isles," printed 1753. 8vo. is a meagre compilation to favour the herring fishery just then established; and of the same stamp is the " exact and authentic account of the greatest white herring fishery in Scotland, carried on yearly in the island of Zetland by the Dutch only, 1750," 8vo.

To complete the Topography of the Northern parts of the kingdom, Mr, Pennant supported the Rev. Mr. George Low, minister of Birsa, Orkney, in a voyage through the Orkney and Zetland Isles [in 1774]. He transmitted to him the MS. account of his voyage, which is executed in a very satisfactory manner. He enters largely into the state of the fisheries and commercial concerns of the islands, and gives a very good account of their antiquities. Mr. Pennant means to complete the voyages of our islands, by publishing, at his own expense, this work of Mr. Low, and should any profits arise, dedicate them to his benefit.[1]

The oldest map of Orkney and Zetland is that by Timothy Pont.

One captain West, who about 1730 or 1734, was wrecked upon the coast of Shetland, and lived there some time, made a map or chart of it; but, besides that it was very imperfect and borrowed from Dutch charts, it does not appear to have been engraved.

Captain Preston, before mentioned, made a new survey in 1743 and 1744. The places where he was are exactly laid down; but in those copied from former charts the mistakes are retained. This chart has many marginal notes, and is sold by Mount and Page on Tower-hill.

From the scanty and imperfect accounts hitherto given of this cluster of islands dependant on the British crown, which Mr. Camden [2] before the Union thought no better

---

[1] [This work, under the title of " A Tour thro' the Islands of Orkney and Schetland," has now been printed for the first time, with an Introduction by JOSEPH ANDERSON, Editor of the Translation of the " Orkneyinga Saga," etc., and published by William Peace & Son, Kirkwall, 1879, 8vo.]

[2] *Schetlandia*, quæ nonnullis *Hethlandia*, est insula aliis exiguis corónata sub imperio Scotorum *frigore obrigens et undique procellis exposita*, cujus incolis perinde ut *Islandia* piscis exsiccatus et contusus pro farre est. Britannia, p. 850, Ed. 1607.

in point of situation and advantages than Iceland and its
inhabitants, a parcel of frozen Ichthypophagi, it is no un-
fair presumption that a more minute detail, written by a
native and a resident little more than 50 years ago (so
slowly does knowledge and information travel) would not
be unacceptable, at a time when the BRITISH FISHERIES
are become so much the object of public attention.[1]

*The following information relative to the author of this
      work came to hand after the preceding pages were
      printed.*

" THE Gifford family of Busta in Shetland, or Zetland,
have been proprietors and possessed of great property
there. The estate at present, including the fisheries, yields
above £1200 yearly, which has arisen to that sum by fishing and wrecks. There is a traditional report, that in the
year 1739, or 1740, when the earl of Morton visited this
family, Mr. Gifford told the earl, that there was a Swedish
East India ship wrecked near his house, and that his fishers,
among other articles got from that ship, found on the
coast, a large log of lead, which his servants used as a stool
in his kitchen. This his lordship viewed, and scraping a
part of it with a knife, informed him that it was silver,
and was the most valuable piece of furniture in the house.
    It was afterwards taken care of, and sold for the benefit
of the owners, after paying the salvage.
    The late Mr. Gifford of Busta was a very respectable
gentleman, generous to his tenants and servants, and a
very useful member of society. His lady was sister to
the late Sir Andrew Mitchell of Westshore. The present laird's grandfather had three sons, who were lost in
a boat crossing a bay in the month of June, 1746. His
father was not then born; he succeeded to the grandfather's estate on his decease. It is remarked, that the
Morton family got the superiorities of Orkney and Zetland,

1 See Mr. James Anderson's " Account of the Present State of the Hebrides
and Western coasts of Scotland," just published [1785], in 8vo,

                                                      which

which belonged to the earls of Orkney, after his forfeiture, as a pledge for £30,000, which his predecessors had advanced to the Royal Family during the reigns of queen Mary, James VI., and Charles I., which was granted to James earl of Morton in the year 1741 or 1742, by king George II. in a perpetual free gift, and in 1767 was sold for £63,000 to Sir Laurence Dundas, whose son now inherits that property. The present laird is Gideon Gifford, of Busta, esquire.

A

DESCRIPTION

OF

ZETLAND

CHAPTER I.

Containing a Geographical Description of the Isles of Zetland, in 1733; its Extent, and Divisions into Parishes.

THE Island of ZETLAND lies about 20 leagues N.E. from the Orkneys, between 60 and 61 degrees N. latitude, and longitude between 2 and 3 W. from London, having the German Ocean on the east, the Ducalidonian Ocean on the west and north, and the sea that divides it from the Orkneys on the south. It consisting of 33 inhabited islands, many whereof are very small and inconsiderable; containing some one, and others two or three poor families. The whole island together is in length, from north to south, 64 miles; and in breadth from east to west, 36 miles where broadest; and is divided into 27 Parishes, many whereof being very small, two or three of them is united into one parish; each of these united parishes being a bailifvic, and the charge of one minister of the Gospel, being in all 12 parishes, (besides a new erection of Fair isle, Foully, and Skeries), in the following order:

The

The whole inhabited Islands are,

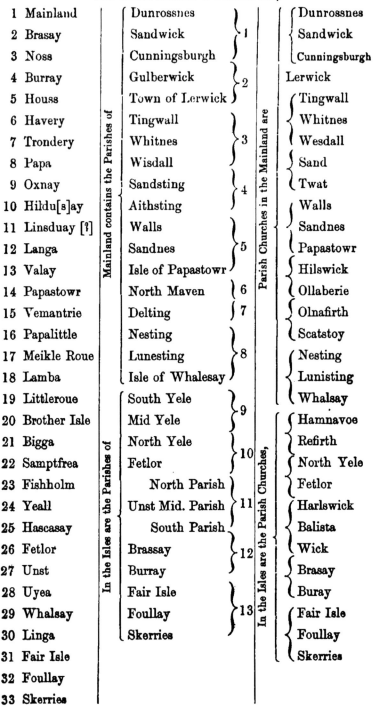

#	Island	Mainland contains the Parishes of		Parish Churches in the Mainland are
1	Mainland	Dunrossnes	} 1	Dunrossnes
2	Brasay	Sandwick		Sandwick
3	Noss	Cunningsburgh		Cunningsburgh
4	Burray	Gulberwick	} 2	Lerwick
5	Houss	Town of Lerwick		Tingwall
6	Havery	Tingwall	} 3	Whitnes
7	Trondery	Whitnes		Wesdall
8	Papa	Wisdall		Sand
9	Oxnay	Sandsting	} 4	Twat
10	Hildu[s]ay	Aithsting		Walls
11	Linsduay [?]	Walls	} 5	Sandnes
12	Langa	Sandnes		Papastowr
13	Valay	Isle of Papastowr		Hilswick
14	Papastowr	North Maven	} 6	Ollaberie
15	Vemantrie	Delting	} 7	Olnafirth
16	Papalittle	Nesting		Scatstoy
17	Meikle Roue	Lunesting	} 8	Nesting
18	Lamba	Isle of Whalesay		Lunisting

#	Island	In the Isles are the Parishes of		In the Isles are the Parish Churches,
19	Littleroue	South Yele	} 9	Whalsay
20	Brother Isle	Mid Yele		Hamnavoe
21	Bigga	North Yele	} 10	Refirth
22	Samptfrea	Fetlor		North Yele
23	Fishholm	North Parish	} 11	Fetlor
24	Yeall	Unst Mid. Parish		Harlswick
25	Hascasay	South Parish		Balista
26	Fetlor	Brassay	} 12	Wick
27	Unst	Burray		Brasay
28	Uyea	Fair Isle	} 13	Buray
29	Whalsay	Foullay		Fair Isle
30	Linga	Skerries		Foullay
31	Fair Isle			Skerries
32	Foullay			
33	Skerries			

Zetland is thus divided into twelve parishes, besides the new erection of Fair Isle, Foully, and Skery, which did formerly belong, Fair Isle to the parish of Dunrosnes, Foully to the parish of Walls, and Skery to the parish of Nesting, and the tythes payable yearly out of them do still belong to the vicars of these parishes.

The biggest island of Zetland is that called the *Mainland*, being in length, from north to south, about 48 miles; and in breadth, from east to west, 20 miles where broadest; but is so much indented with bays of the sea on all sides, called here *Voes*, that there is not any part of it two miles from the sea on one side or the other. It contains eight parishes.

First, The united parishes of *Dunrosnes, Sandwick*, and *Cuningsburg*, in length, from north to south, 16 miles; and about three miles broad where broadest; surrounded with the sea except on the north; bounded by Quarfs in Gulberwick, Sandwick, and Cuningsburg. It is for the most part high mountains, covered with heath and marshes, the arable ground being all upon the sea coast. Dunrosnes is the southermost part of Zetland, and is mostly low ground and sandy downs, excepting two promontories; the one called *Fitfall-head*, and the other *Samburg-head*. There is a good deal of arable ground in these parishes, but much of it is overblown with the sand and lost. They have very little pasture ground in this parish, so they have very few sheep; but in Cuningsburg they have plenty of them. They have cows, oxen, and horses, but do not make so much butter for exportation as in the other parishes of the country. Most of the inhabitants are fishers; they catch abundance of small fish to feed upon, a few cod and ling for export; but their principal fishing is that of Scath, which they take in that rapid current that runs off Samburg-head, called the *Roust*, which sets away north west with the ebb, and south east with the flood; and when the tide sets against the wind, the waves run very high and break, which is dangerous, and often fatal to the poor fishermen, who use only small yawls, and but few men in each. The scath has a large fat liver, of which they make

oil:

oil: the fish is salted and dried and sold at Dundee and Leith. This parish is not so well provided with good harbours for ships as the rest of the country; on the west side of it there is none, save one at *Bigtown* only safe in summer; on the south is *Quindall-bay*, an open place, where a ship can ride safe in summer; on the east near Samburg-head is *Grootness-voe*, where ships usually lie; and a little west from that is another harbour called *The Pool*, where small ships can lie aground upon clean sand; north from that four miles is another bay, called the *Levanwick*, a good summer harbour; six miles further is a good safe place called *Aithsvoe*, having but a narrow entry. This is reckoned the most populous parish in Zetland, and contains about 1750 marks of land. It is thought too great a charge for one minister, and there are tithes enough in it to pay two; but a disjunction cannot be easily obtained, because the vicar of the parish is the greatest heretor in it, without whose consent it cannot be done. There are in this parish three churches; one at Dunrosnes, one at Sandwick, and one at Cuningsburg; but the minister preaches for ordinary only at the two former of these; he has for stipend 800 merks Scots a year; and a glebe and manse. In this, as also in all the parishes of Zetland, there are several old buildings, called *Pights-Houses*, which I shall have occasion to mention afterwards. There are several holms belonging to this parish, only used for pasture of little value, save one called Moussy, in which is one of these Pights houses, a great part whereof is yet standing, called *The Castle of Moussy*. This holm or island is about a mile long, but not broad. It lies to the east of Sandwick. There has been some arable ground in it, but it is now only used for pasture. There are rabbits in it, and also in many places of this parish.

The second parish is that of *Gulberwick*, having Cuningsburg on the south, Tingwall on the west, the sea on the north and east. It is about five miles long from north to south, and two miles broad; all mountains covered with heath, and several fresh water lakes. It is a very small

parish

parish, having in it only about 330 marks of land, including quarfs. It did formerly belong to the parish of Tingwall, but is of late joined to the town of Lerwick, not formally but casually. The arable ground lying near the sea, the inhabitants are all fishers, mostly of small fish, for themselves to feed upon; they also catch a few cod and ling for export. They have oxen, cows, sheep, and horses; milk and butter in summer. On the east side of this parish stands the town of Lerwick, upon a small bay of the sea, covered with the island of Brasy, which forms a fine large road, very commodious for ships to ride in at all seasons of the year. It is more frequented by foreigners, especially the Dutch, than any other place in Zetland, and is called by them the *Buss-Haven*, the Dutch-herring buss fleet having always made that the place of their rendezvous before they begin the herring fishing, ever since their first entry upon that trade, it being a very convenient place for them to repair their ships when leaky, or to take in fresh water, and they can sail out with any wind, the road having an entry to the south, and another to the north that leads into the sea. They come yearly about the ninth or tenth of June, and lie till the 13th, upon which day they must begin their fishing, and not sooner. I have seen some old men who said that they have seen in Brasy Sound, at one time, 2200 busses; but these 40 years past there never was above 5 or 600 of them in at once; and in anno 1702, the French burned about 150 of them in Brasy Sound, and along the coast, since which time there never was above 3 or 400 of them in at once. These Dutchmen used formerly to buy a considerable quantity of coarse stockings from the country people, for ready money, at a tolerable good price, by which a good deal of foreign money was annually imported, which enabled the poor inhabitants to pay the land rent, and to purchase the necessaries of life; but for several years past that trade has failed, few or none of these busses coming in, and those that come, if they buy a few stockings, it is at a very low price, whereby the country people are become exceeding poor, and unable to pay the land rent. The town of *Lerwick* was built upon account of

foreigners

foreigners frequenting that place. I have known old men who remembered when there was not one house there; but now there are about 200 families in it, abundance of good houses, and fashionable people as are to be seen in any town of Scotland of its bulk. At the north end of the town there is a regular fort built at the charge of the government, in the reign of king Charles II. In the time of his first war with the Dutch his Majesty was pleased to send over here a garrison consisting of 300 men, under the command of one colonel William Sinclair, a native of Zetland; and one Mr. Milne, architector for building the said fort, with 20 or 30 cannons, to plant upon it for the protection of the country. There was a house built within the fort sufficient to lodge 100 men; the garrison staid here three years; the charge whereof, with the building of the fort, is said to stand the king 28,000 pounds sterling. When the garrison removed, they carried off the cannon from the fort, and in the next war with the Dutch 2 or 3 years after the garrison removed, a Dutch frigate came into Brasy Sound, and burnt the house in the fort, and several others, the best in the town of Lerwick; and that in the fort was never repaired since. In the late war with France, the French privateers came into Brasy Sound, and round the whole islands at their pleasure, we having no force to hold them off. They were a more generous enemy than the Dutch, doing little damage to the country, sometimes demanding some fresh provisions, which were readily given them; we being in no condition to keep them off were glad to purchase their friendship at so easy a rate. The town of Lerwick has no freedoms nor privileges, but is governed by a baillie upon the same footing with the other baillies in the country. There is a church in it, and one minister of the gospel, who is now minister of Lerwick and Gulberwick. He has for stipend 500 marks, paid him out of the bishop's rents of Orkney, 300 marks by the town of Lerwick, and the tythes of Gulberwick about 200 marks; making in all 1,000 marks Scots yearly, with a free house and yard. As Lerwick chiefly subsists by the resort of foreigners to it, so when that fails it must decline, as indeed

deed it has done for several years past, having been very little frequented by foreigners, and thereby is become very poor. Several projects have been talked of and written upon of late, that might have been very beneficial to Lerwick and Zetland had they taken place ; as that of the British merchants carrying goods from Muscovy and Sweden designed for the plantations in America, that must be entered in Britain, could have them entered at Lerwick, which would save a great deal of time and charges to these merchants ; also the Greenland and Herring Fishery Companies of Britain proposed Lerwick as a most commodious port for lodging their stores in, and for repacking their herrings, melting their oil, and thence exporting the same to foreign markets. The grand objection of these settlements is, that Lerwick is an open unfortified place, and in case of a war the merchants ships and goods would be exposed to the enemy ; for removing of which difficulty, would the government bestow a small garrison upon it of only 100 men and about 20 pieces of cannon, and be at a small charge in repairing the old fort, and erecting a small battery or two more, that might be sufficient to secure the place against any ordinary effort the enemy might make against it ; and Lerwick being thus fortified, all British ships coming from the East or West Indies could come safely there in time of war, and lye secure until carried thence by convoy, or otherways as the proprietors should direct ; and thus Lerwick might become more advantageous to the trade of Great Britain than Gibraltar or Port Mahon ; and that for one-tenth part of the charge of either of those places to the Government.

3d. The united parishes of *Tingwall, Whitnes,* and *Wisdall,* which are about eight miles long from south to north, and five miles broad, having the islands of Frondray and Burray on the south, Gulberwick on the east, Nesting and Delting on the north, and Artsling on the west. It is for the most part mountains covered with heath, and many fresh-water lakes ; in the valleys is some arable and grass ground. This united parish is about 1500 marks of land. Most of the inhabitants are fishers ; they

catch

catch a few cod and ling for export, and abundance of small fish for food. They have oxen, cows, sheep, horses, and some swine, milk and butter, for paying the land rent. On the south-side of the parish of Tingwall is a small village called *Scallaway*, upon a bay of the sea, covered with the island of Frondray, and it is a very good safe harbour for ships, but little frequented by any. At the east end of the village stands the old house built by Patrick Stuart, earl of Orkney, called the Castle of Scallaway, of which now nothing remains but the stone walls; it has been a very handsome tower-house, with fine vaulted cellars and kitchen, with a well in it, a beautiful spacious entry, with a turret upon each corner, and large windows, all grated with iron, which is now all rusted away; over the entry-gate is the following inscription, cut in stone:

PATRICIUS STEUARDUS ORCHADIÆ ET ZETLANDIÆ
COMES. I. V. R S.
CUJUS FUNDAMEN SAXUM EST, DOM'ILLA MANEBIT
LABILIS E CONTRA SI SIT ARENA PERIT
A. D. 1600.

It is said, that in building this house Earl Patrick did exceedingly oppress the country, by laying a tax upon each parish thereof, whereby they were obliged to find as many men as was needed to serve in the work, and provisions for all the workmen during the work, without a farthing charge to the Earl; and if any was found deficient, they were punished by forfeiting their whole goods. This little town of Scallaway is much more ancient than Lerwick, and was their usual seat of justice; and all public letters are still executed at the castle of Scallaway, but the head courts are now commonly kept at Lerwick, where the heritors can be better accommodated than at Scallaway, where there are not now above twenty small families, besides two or three gentlemen's seats. Scallaway stands about four miles W. S. W. from Lerwick. Four miles N. from Scallaway is *Laxfrith*, a fine harbour for ships; on the East side of the country,
half

half a mile East from that, is another bay called *Deals Voe;* betwixt Scallaway and Laxfrith is a pleasant strath or valley betwixt two hills, for the most part arable and grass ground, in the middle whereof stands the church of *Tingwall,* and the minister's manse hard by it, nigh whereunto is a lake called the Lough of Tingwall, at the north end whereof is a small plot of ground surrounded with water, and a bridge of a few rough stones piled together to go upon it, called the *Lawtainy.* Here it is said the head courts were kept of old time, where all the Udillers were obliged to convene when called by the forvd or ship magistrate, and coming all on horseback, they had their horses grased in the neighbourhood thereof, for which it is said, that the proprietors of Grista and Astar (two adjacent rooms) to make up their damage, had, the former the seat of some lands in Wisdall and Eastershild, and the latter the seat of Quarf and half the seat of Cuningsburg, which continues to this day in the possession of those deriving right from them. Two miles west from Tingwall is a bay of the sea called the *Voe of Restanes;* and a little west from that is another bay called the *Voe of Binanes;* and a quarter of a mile N. W. from that is another bay called the *Voe of Wisdall.* There were formerly in this united parish three churches, one at Tingwall, one at Whitnes, and one at Wisdall: but of late those old churches of Whitnes and Wisdall are laid aside, and there is a new church built betwixt the two; these united parishes also including Gulberwick, the islands of Trondray, Oxnay and Hildory, was an archdeanrie, and the archdean had right to all the tythes and kirk-lands in that parish, so that the bishop had nothing paid him thereout; which at last falling into the hands of a lay gentleman, he paid the minister of Tingwall nearly 6 or 700 marks of stipend, with the glebe and manor of Tingwall; but that family failing, who were proprietors of the tythes and vicar of the parish, those to whom they had been made over not taking care to pay the minister's stipend, he, with concurrence of the heritors, made application to the lords for plantation of kirk and valisation of tythes, who gave

orders

orders to the minister to uplift as much of the tythes of
the parish as paid him his stipend, at the rate of 900 merks
yearly : and also for 200 merks out of the tythes of Gulberwick, to the minister of Lerwick, which they have uplifted for several years bygone ; and the proprietor or vicar
has not yet appeared to claim his property therein.

4th. Is the united parishes of *Sandsting* and *Aithsting*,
being about eight miles long from north to south, and about
seven miles broad when broadest, but much indented with
bays of the sea, having Wisdall on the east, Delting and
the sea on the north, Walls and Sandness on the west, and
the sea on the south. It is for the most part mountains
and marshes covered with heath ; and has many lakes and
burns ; the arable and grass ground is upon the sea-coast,
containing about 740 marks of land. This parish is but
thinly inhabited ; the mountains serves for pasture to sheep
and horses ; they have cows and oxen, milk and butter ;
most of the inhabitants are fishers, who take a few cod and
ling for export, and small fish for themselves to eat. On
the east of this parish is a bay of the sea, called *Bixater
Voe*, that runs up north-west about six miles into the
country, a fine harbour, but seldom or never frequented by
any ships. A little to the south thereof, the *Voe of Sana*,
and a little to the west thereof is *Sarla Voe*. Three miles
south from that is *Shilda Voe ;* and on the west of this
parish is a long bay of the sea, called *Grutten Voe*, running
about six miles up into the country ; on the north of it is
Aiths Voe, and *Brimster Voe*, also *Kilingster Voe*, all good
harbours for ships, but seldom or never used by any. Inhabited islands belonging to this parish are *Vemantrie*,
lying on the north of it, a small place with only one small
family upon it ; and about two miles east from that is
another small island, called *Papa Littte*, one poor family
upon it ; there are two churches, one at Sana in Sanasting,
the other at Tival in Aithsting. The minister is vicar of
the parish, and has for stipend half of the corn tythes, and
the whole vicarage tythes amounting to above seven hundred merks Scots per annum, with a glebe and manse.

5th. The united parishes of *Walls, Sandness,* and *Papastowr.*

stowr. Walls and Sandness is about six miles long from
north to south, and about 4 miles broad, having Aithsting
and Sandsting on the east, and the sea on the south, west,
and north. It is all mountains covered with heath; the
arable and grass ground being on the skirts of it upon the
sea coast, amounting to about 626 mark land. The island of
Papastowr lies about two miles west from Sandness, is about
three miles long, and two miles broad, has in it 216 marks
of land. On the south of Walls is a small island called
Valay, which has in it only 24 marks of arable land. Betwixt this island and Walls is a good harbour, called *Valay
Sound.* In this parish there are oxen, cows, sheep, and
horses; they have milk and butter; most of the inhabitants
are fishers; they catch a few ling, cod, and herrings, for
export, and plenty of small fish to feed upon; in this
united parish are three churches, one in Walls, one in
Sandness, and one in Papa; the minister thereof has for
stipend half of the corn tythes, and the whole vicarage
tythes amounting to about 800 marks per annum, with a
glebe and manse.

6th. The parish of *Northaven,* about 16 miles long
from south to north, and about 8 marks broad where
broadest. It is a peninsula, surrounded with the sea save
only on the south. It is joined to the parish of Delting
by a small neck of land about 40 yards over, called *Mavis-
Grind.* This is the largest parish in Zetland, but not the
most populous; it is all mountains, covered with heath and
marshes; a vast many lakes and burns abounding with
trouts; all the arable and grass ground is on the skirts of
it along the sea-coast, extending to about 1150 marks of
land. One mountain in this parish is remarkable for its
height, from the top whereof, the horizon being clear, one
may see round the whole islands of Zetland; it is called
Roneshill, and is often covered with snow when there is
none any where else in Zetland. The inhabitants of this
parish are for the most part fishers; they take cod, ling,
and some herrings, for export, and abundance of small fish
to feed upon; they have cows, oxen, sheep, horses, and a
few swine, milk and butter. On the east-side of this

parish

parish is a small bay of the sea, running up south about eight miles, dividing betwixt the parishes of Delting and Northaven, all good anchor-ground, but very little frequented by ships. A little north from that is another fine harbour, called *Gluss Voe*. North thereof another, called *Ullaberse* Farther north is *Quefrith Voe*; and north of that *Callafrith Voe*. Yet farther north is *Rurra Voe*; all on the east-side of the parish. On the north-west is a bay, called *Sand Voe*; and on the south side of Roneshill is a fine bay called *Runis Voe*, running up 4 or 5 miles into the land. South from that 3 miles is a bay called *Humna Voe*. On the south-west side of this parish is the bay, called *Illsweek Voe*, upon the north-side of the great bay, called *St. Magnus Bay*; and east from that 2 miles is a small bay, called *Hamers Voe*. Farther south 2 miles, is *Gunasiter Voe*, and three miles south from that is *Ilsburgh Voe*; a quarter of a mile south from that is a small bay, called *Culsiter Minn*, on the west side of Mavis Grind. In this parish are two churches, that on the west-side at Hilswick, on the east that of Ottaberse; the minister of this parish is vicar, having right to the whole vicarage-tythes thereof, and half of the corn-tythes, and it is worth about 1000 merks per annum, with a glebe and manse. Inhabited islands belonging to this parish is only a very small one, called *Lamby*, on the east thereof; one family upon it.

7th. The parish of *Delting* being ten miles long from north to south, and six miles broad. It has Gelsound and Northaven on the north, the sea on the west, Aithsting and Wisdall on the south, Nesting and Lunesting on the east. It is all mountains covered with heath and marshes, a great many lakes and burns stored with trouts; the arable ground is along the sea-coast, extending to about 870 marks of land; many of the inhabitants are fishers, mostly of small fish, such as pillocks and sellocks, of whose livers they make a good deal of oil some years, especially those who live about Yelsound, where there goes a rapid tide, in which these fish delight most to swim, and there they are fattest. There are very few fishers of cod and ling for export here. They have cows, oxen, sheep, horses, and

and some swine, milk and butter. Inhabited islands belonging to this parish are those of *Meikle Roo*, in which are four or five small families on the west side of the parish. On the north thereof is *Little Roo*, one family on it; *Brother Isle*, a very small isle; *Biga*, a small isle; *Picholina*, one family upon it. There are in this parish two churches, one at Scalsla, the other at Olnafrith. The minister is vicar of the parish, and has for stipend all the vicarage tythes, and half the corn tythes, and it is about 800 merks Scots a year.

8th. The united parishes of *Nesting, Lunesting*, and island of *Whaley*. Nesting and Lunesting is 9 miles long from north to south, and 4 miles broad where broadest, but very unequally. It is all mountains and mosses, many fresh-water lakes and burns, with plenty of trouts in them; the inhabitants are for the most part fishers, as they are also in the island of Whaley, which is three miles long and a mile broad, mostly moore-ground; the arable land is upon the sea coast. This island contains about 220 marks of land, as Nesting and Lunesting do 510 marks of land. There is some ling and cod caught here for export, and plenty of small fish; they have cows, oxen, sheep, horses, and some swine, milk and butter. In this parish are three churches, one in Nesting, one in Lunesting, and one in Whaley. The minister is vicar of the parish, having for stipend the whole vicarage-tythes, and half the corn tythes, amounting to about 800 merks a year, with a glebe and manse. Inhabited island belonging to this parish is a small one nigh Whaley, called *Linga;* one small family upon it. *Skery* also belongs to this parish, but is now joined to Fairisle and Foully. These eight parishes lie upon the main land of Zetland.

9th. The island of *Yeall*, sixteen miles long, and 6 miles broad where broadest, lies about one mile north from Delting, is for the most part all mountains and mosses, and is divided into the parishes of *South Yeall, Mid Yeall*, and *North Yeall*, the two former being united in one parish, and the latter joined to the island of Fetlor. South and Mid Yeall contains about 1017 marks of arable land, which lie all

all in the skirts of it along the sea shore.   The inhabitants are for the most part fishers ; they take some ling and cod for export, and plenty of small fish to feed upon : they have cows, oxen, sheep, and horses, milk and butter.   In Mid Yeall, upon the east-side, is a small bay, called *Refirth Voe*, a good safe harbour for ships ; on the east-side, half-a-mile west from that, is a bay called *Whalefirth Voe*, which leads out to the west sea, and also a good harbour, but seldom or never used.   In South Yeall, upon the east side is *Bura Voe*, a very safe small harbour ; two miles west from that is *Hamna Voe*, a good harbour ; and four miles west from that is *Leadie Voe*, a good harbour.   In this parish are two churches, one at Hamna Voe in South Yeall, the other at Refirth in Mid Yeall.   Inhabited islands belonging to this parish are *Hascosie*, a small island on the east side, one family on it ; and *Samphra* on the south, a small island, two or three poor families upon it.   The minister is vicar of the parish, and has for stipend all the vicarage tythes, and half the corn tythes, which is about 800 merks a year, and a glebe and manse.

10. The united parishes of *North Yeall* and *Fetlor*.   The island of Fetlor is about 4 miles long, and 3 miles broad where broadest ; it lies about two miles east from Yeall ; it is for the most part dry bare ground ; there is in it 784 marks of arable land, all sixpenny land ; the inhabitants are for the most part fishers, they take ling and cod for export, and plenty of small fish for food ; they have oxen and cows, but few sheep and horses, having little pasture-ground ; they have abundance of milk and butter.   North Yeall contains 640 marks of arable land ; the inhabitants are mostly fishers, they catch ling and cod for export, and abundance of small fish to feed upon ; they have oxen, cows, sheep, and horses, milk and butter ; on the north east is a small bay called *Bulla Voe*, a safe place for ships ; four miles farther south is another bay, called *Celles Firth Voe*, a safe place for ships.   In Fetlor there is no safe harbour.   There was formerly a lay vicar here, and this parish belonged to Yeall ; but in 1713 it was disjoined, with the consent of the gentleman who had right to the vicarage,

who

who was allowed as many years of the tythes as paid the sum he laid out in the purchase of it, and now the minister of this parish is vicar himself, and has for stipend all the vicarage tythes, and half of the corn tythes, extending to about 800 merks a year; he has two churches, one at North Yeall, and one in Fetlor.

11. The island of *Unst*. This is the northmost of all the British islands. It is eight miles long and four miles broad; it lies a mile north-east from Yeall, in the Sound or Straight betwixt which, called *Bluma Sound*, runs a very rapid tide, setting away north with the ebb, and south with the flood, as all the tides about Zetland do; but in all these Sounds or Straights betwixt the islands there are two or three tides running contrary to one another, as when the great current in the middle of the Sound sets north, then there is a tide at each shore, called the Edy-tide, that sets as fast south, and so shifts about as the great current alters. At the north point of this island, called *Ska*, goes a very rapid current, like the Roust of Samburg-head, wherein also there swim plenty of that fish called Scath; but the fishers here have not the way of catching them. This island of Unst is somewhat plainer than the other isles of Zetland, and is for the most part dry bare ground, very rocky, and is divided into the *south mall* and *north* parishes, and contains about 2050 marks of land, all cheap land, 6 pennies the mark, and generally it is improven. The inhabitants are for the most part fishers; they catch ling and cod for export, and abundance of small fish for food. They have oxen, cows, some sheep, and plenty of very little horses; they have milk and butter for paying the land-rent. On the east of Unst is an island called *Baltay*, in which there has been some arable ground, but it is now only used for pasture. It covers a fine bay called *Balta-sound*, and a good safe harbour. On the south is another island called *Uyor*, containing 84 marks of arable land, and one family upon it. It covers a bay called *Uyor Sound*, a good road for ships. In this parish are three churches; that in the south parish is the church of *Wick*, in the mid parish is the church of *Balista*, in the north parish that of

Harlswick,

Harlswick, and one minister. There is a lay-vicar, who pays the minister a yearly stipend of 900 merks; he has also a glebe and manse.

12. The islands of *Brasy* and *Burray;* the one lying on the east, and the other on the west side of the main island, at about six miles distant from each other. Brasy lies east from the town of Lerwick about a mile. It is three miles long from north to south, and two miles broad. It is somewhat mountainous, mostly covered with heath and moss. The arable ground is on the skirts of it, extending to 294 marks of land. The inhabitants are mostly fishers; they catch ling and cod for export and small fish to eat; they have oxen and cows, a few sheep and horses, milk and butter. There are in this island two little old churches laid aside, and one new church, lately built more convenient. There is a small island belonging to Brasy, lying on the east thereof, called *Noss,* in which are 60 marks of arable land, and two or three families. On the the north side of Brasy is a small bay called *Aiths Voe,* a good harbour. Burray is about three miles long, one broad; it is mostly dry bare ground; the arable ground is along the sea-shore, extending to 192 marks of land. The island of *Houss* thereto belonging is about two miles long, contains about 60 marks of arable land, and there are four families on it. Another small island thereto belonging, called *Havery,* has two families on it. Betwixt the islands of Houss and Burray is a good harbour for ships. To the east of Houss is a long bay called *Clift Sound,* also a good harbour. There is a church in Burray; the minister of Brasy and Burray is vicar of these islands, and has for stipend all the vicarage tythes, and half the corn-tythes, which amounts to about 700 merks per annum.

13. The new-erected parishes of *Fair Isle, Foully,* and *Skery* are very small, but the most discontiguous parish in Britain. Fair Isle is a small island about two miles long, one broad; it lies about eight leagues south from Samburghead, contains 96 marks of good arable ground. The inhabitants are all fishers, they catch ling, cod, and scath, and plenty of small fish. There is a small bay on the north

side

side of it, where boats or small barks can ride safe; they
have some oxen, cows, and a few sheep. Foully lies twelve
leagues north-west from the Fair Isle. It is a small but
very high island. There are in it 54 marks of arable land,
and some grass ground. The inhabitants are fishers, they
catch cod and ling, and abundance of small fish. They
have great plenty of sea-fowls, that nestle in the high rocks
of the island, and many of the inhabitants are dexterous
in climbing these rocks to take the young fowls before
they can fly, but often lose their lives by falling over the
rocks into the sea. On the north-east side of the island
is a small bay, where any small vessel can lie safe in summer. They have some cows, and sheep. Skery lies 20
leagues north-east from the Fair Isle. It is composed of
three very small islands, lying near each other in a tri-
angle, which forms three small entries to a little safe harbour in the middle of them. The biggest island is called
Houssy; the other *Browary;* and the third *Grunay.* The
two former are inhabited; the first containing 36, and the
other 18 marks of arable land; the inhabitants are all
fishers; they catch some ling and cod for export, and abundance of small fish to feed upon. They have a few cows and
sheep. There is a little church at Fair Isle, one at Foully,
and one in Skery; the minister thereof resides at Fair
Isle and visits Foully and Skery once a year, staying in
each of them a week or two, and then returns to his common residence. He has his stipend paid him by the
general assembly of the church of Scotland, out of the fund
allowed by the king for defraying the charge of the assembly; his stipend is only 400 merks Scots a year, which
is little enough considering his travel and dangerous passage.

CHAPTER II.

Of the first Inhabitants of ZETLAND, *and its Name.*

WHEN these islands were first inhabited, or by whom,
we have no certain account. Some think the Pights, or

Picts,

Picts, were the first inhabitants ; others, the Norwegians : however, it is certain, both did inhabit them, but at what time, or how long they were possessed by the Pights, I could never see any such account thereof as is much to be depended on; however peremptorily asserted by some of our old Scotish historians, who talk of a long succession of the Pights, kings of Orkney and Zetland. But whatever may be in that, there are some such vestiges remaining to this day as sufficiently prove that the Pights did possess Orkney and Zetland ; as that of a vast many old buildings, called Pights houses, of which here are several yet to be seen in every parish in Zetland ; many of them one or two stories high, yet standing, and they are all built after one form, that is, round, of large rough stones, very well laid ; but these buildings are not alike great, some of them not twenty feet diameter, others thirty feet within the wall, which is ten or twelve feet thick, the heart whereof is all little apartments and stairs ; they have had no windows, and a very little entry door. Whether they have been roofed at top or not does not appear, but they have all been built in the most inaccessable places, such as surrounded with water, or upon some high rock, and some have two or three walls of earth and stone round them ; and they are still known by the name of Pights houses, or burghs. Now *burgh*, in the Teutonic language, signifies a castle or fort, as *Pight* derived from *Pfightan*, another word in that language, signifying to *fight*, or *fighters ;* and these Pights are said to come from Germany, and to have spoken that language ; and all these Pights houses are so situate within sight of each other, that by a signal of fire or smoke they could alarm the whole country in less than one hour of the approach of the enemy, or any other danger. But at what time, or how long these Pights did possess Orkney and Zetland is still uncertain.

That the Norwegians did long possess the island of Orkney and Zetland is uncontrovertible; but that they were the first discoverers of these islands (as some would have them) is very doubtful. That which seems most to favour the Norwegian's pretension is, that the names of

the

the islands and places in them are all Danish, and continue so for the most part to this day ; and the customs. manners, and language of the old Zetlanders, with their way of living, were the same as in Norway, even down to the time of some old men yet living ; and the greatest part of the vulgar inhabitants, and some of considerable note here, still reckon themselves of Danish extract, and are all Patronymics, whereby they are distinguished from those that have come from the continent of Britain, who have all surnames, and have for many years past been the most considerable, though the least numerous. Still these old Danish inhabitants value themselves much upon their antiquity, and scorn to take surnames as a novelty unknown to their fore fathers ; particularly one Patrik Gilbertson, of Ilsburgh, an old man about ninety years, alive at writing hereof, reckons himself the 22d generation, in a lineal succession, possessors of Ilsburgh, stiled Patronymics ; and many more here that account themselves of very long standing. But, however far the names of places, customs, language, and traditions of the old Zetland inhabitants may go to prove them of Norwegian extract, yet considering the affinity of the language spoken by the Pights, and that spoken by the Norwegians, being both of Teutonic original, as also that of their customs and manners, being so near neighbours, I think the Pights stand as fair to be the first inhabitants of Orkney and Zetland, as the Norwegians, and therefore shall leave them to share that honour betwixt them, and allow the ancient inhabitants to be equally descended from both, and I know not by which they have the most honour. So much for the first inhabitants of Zetland. In the next place I shall a little consider its name.

These islands are known in our English language by the name of *Zetland*. They are called in Dutch *Hetlandt ;* by the Danes and Norwegians, *Yetlandt.* Without naming any more languages, as nothing to the purpose, the name appears plainly to be of Teutonic or Gothic original ; for the Dutch name *Hetlandt* is made up of two words, as *het* signifies *called* or *named,* and *landt* is *land,* which in

English

English may be rendered *called land,* or *a land.* The Danish name also is two words, *yet* and *landt,* the first signifying the number *one* or *a,* and the other *land,* which two words may be expressed *an land,* or *a land*; nay, even the English name of it also contains two words, if it be allowed that the letter Z was not many years since used for Y in our writings, and then it would be pronounced *Yetland,* by which it would seem that the first discoverers, having found Orkney sailing north, he who first saw Zetland called out *Yetland,* or *a land,* which became the common name of those islands. This to me appears the most probable conjecture, leaving others at liberty to find out a better etymology thereof at their pleasure.

CHAPTER III.

A Description of the Air, Soil, and Product of Zetland.

AIR.] Zetland being very mountainous, abounding with fresh-water lakes and marshes, and surrounded with the sea, is for the most part still covered with fogs, which make the air thick, and therefore not so cold in winter as many other places of a far more southern situation, but unwholsome to breathe in, and occasion frequent fevers, colds, rheums, and scurvey, the common diseases of the country; but the often and exceeding hard gales of wind that blow here help to purify the air, as also in winter, sometimes frosts and snow, which seldom last long, so that it is not very cold here in winter, nor is it oft warm, much less hot in summer, and the air is tolerably healthful.

SOIL.] These islands lying in the 13th north climate, and surrounded with the sea, cannot be thought very fertile; and being all mountains and marshes, so soked with the almost perpetual rains that fall here, especially in the winter season, the ground is kept so cold, that little or nothing can grow out of it, especially the inland part, which is generally all covered with heath and moss; the arable and grass ground is mostly nigh the sea-coast, and

produceth

produceth only small oats, and bear, a kind of barley. In some places there is very good grass-ground and hay; but the people have not the right way of making their hay, nor have they often so much dry weather as to make it good. The arable land in some places here is very good, and yields as much increase in good years as they have in better countries; and the arable ground might be much more improved, but the people are generally taken up about the fishing in summer, and in winter it is bad weather and short days, so there is little to be done without doors. There grow no trees here. In the gentlemen's small gardens grow very good roots, such as turneps, parsneps, carrots, and crurnocks, salet, and all such herbs and flowers as grow in the north of Scotland will grow here, if pains be taken about them; also gooseberries, currants, strawberries, and artichokes. Fruit and barren trees will also grow if fenced with a ditch, and much care taken about them, but seldom come to bear fruit; potatoes grow here, but the people will not be at the pains to plant them; there is plenty of cabbage much used by the inhabitants.

Of the oats and barley that grow here they make meal and malt, but never have so much thereof in the best years as to serve the country; and in bad years not so much as will serve them four or six months in the year; so there are yearly imported from Orkney and Scotland considerable quantities of meal and malt.

There is in several places abundance of limestone, and those places are reckoned the best arable and grass ground; in other places are quarries of free-stone, and in others slate.

There were never any mines discovered yet in these islands; but some are of opinion, that lead and iron mines might be found in some places of them. For fuel they have peat or turf, dug out of the moss the beginning of summer, and dried with the sun, and so put up in stacks for use, some whereof are little inferior to the best coals.

In all these islands are plenty of fresh water springs, besides the lakes and burns.

BEASTS]. In all these islands are oxen and cows of
some-what

some-what larger size than those in Orkney and Caithness; the oxen serve for plowing the ground, and the cows for giving milk, of which they make butter, wherewith most of the land rent is paid, and it is as good as any where else when rightly made; but the people being careless in making the rent butter, it is undervalued at foreign markets, which is a great loss to the country, and some efforts have been used of late to oblige the people to make the butter right, so they begin to make it better. They keep just as many oxen and cows as they can find fodder for in winter.

In many places there is plenty of sheep of a small kind, like those in the north of Scotland, and they might be much more numerous than they are, if care was taken of them as in other places; but they lie summer and winter in the open fields exposed to the rigour of the season, and have no food but what they can find for themselves; and in snowy winters most of them die with hunger and cold. They do not shear the sheep here; but in the month of May their fleece begins to loosen, and then it is pulled off, and against winter another is grown up sufficient to protect them from the cold. Of the sheep-milk they make some butter and cheese, which is not reckoned so good as that of the cows milk; and of the wool they make coarse cloth, stuffs, stockings, &c., but the want of walk-mills is a very great loss to the country, to supply which, and for the encouraging the woollen manufactories there, the right honourable the Earl of Morton has been pleased of late to order a walk-mill to be built at his Lordship's expense, for the benefit of the country; what wool they have more than serves the country is bartered with the Orkney men for stuffs and linnen-cloth yearly.

Here are horses, but of extraordinary small size, some whereof are very pretty and of excellent mettle, and will carry a man over these mountains and mosses, where a large horse could be of no use, and they are otherways very serviceable to the country people, and would be more numerous if any way cared for; but they lie out in the open fields summer and winter, and get no food but what
they

they can find for themselves; so in bad winters many of them die with hunger and cold. It will, no doubt, be wondered at by strangers, that so little care is taken about these sheep and horses which are so useful and beneficial; the reason whereof is, that the poor inhabitants, having used their utmost endeavours, can scarce find food and shelter for their oxen and cows, without which they could not live; and in hard winters many of them die for want of fodder, so they have none to bestow on their sheep and horses, until they find more time to improve the land.

Here are also swine of a small kind, and they might be much more numerous than they are, but, being found very hurtful in turning up and spoiling the grass ground, the people are restricted by a country act to such a small number proportionable to the land they labour, which number they must not exceed. The best mutton and pork here, when rightly fed, is as good as any where else, and there is just as much of it as serves the country, but little or none for export, the reason whereof is, that the common people having little bread, must eat the more flesh, they living more upon fish and flesh than bread.

There are no wild beasts in Zetland, except rabbits, of which there is plenty in many places of the country; nor is their any noxious animal, save the whitred or weasel, who is very hurtful to the rabbits and wildfowls, destroying the young brood in all these islands, or tame fowls, such as hens, geese, and ducks, few of any other kind; wild fowl were much more numerous than now, such as pluvers, whapes, ducks of several kinds, snipes, sterlings, sparrows, larks, and such small birds; wild doves, lapwings, and chalders. There is also here over winter swans, herons, wild geese of several kinds, who all go away in the spring, and return again in autumn. Here is abundance of hawks of different kinds, eagles or erns, corbies, crows, and chalders, or sea piats; many sea fowls, as ember geese, rain geese, scarfes or cormorants, gulmawes, kitiweaks, lires, tarets, &c. Amphibious creatures here are seals and otters. We have no rivers, but a great many burns, or rivulets, well stored with trout, that swim in them from the fresh-
water

water lakes to the sea and again return by them to these lakes at several seasons in the year. There are of those trouts as big as ordinary salmon. Other fresh-water fish here are only eels and flouks or flounders. Salt-water fish round the coast of all these islands are herring in great abundance, in the months of June, July, August, and September; but they are best in June and July; mackrel, ling, cod, fresh haddocks, whitings, turbots, fluiks, skets, conger eels, crowners, and *saith*, which is a large black fish as big as a cod, and the younger sort of these, very small, called *sellocks* and *peltocks* : These small fish are of great use to the country people, who feed upon them most part of the year, and of their livers they make considerable quantity of oil. There is also upon these coasts, at some seasons, vast numbers of *hoas*, a kind of smaller shark, very hurtful to the fisherman's lines and nets; also a big sort of them called *hoaskers*, with skins like shagreen. At some times there come upon these coasts a great many small whales of different kinds, and when falling into a bay, the country people collect as many boats as can be got, and drive them into a creek, and there kill them with scythes, spits, and such other weapons as they can afford. As soon as they are got ashore, the bailie of the parish is advertized, who comes to the place, and takes care that none of them are embezzled; and he acquaints the admiral thereof, who forthwith goes there, and holds a court, where the phiscal presents a petition, narrating the number of whales, how and where drove ashore, and that the judge may give judgment thereupon according to law and the country practice; whereupon the admiral ordains the whales drove on shore to be divided in three equal parts; one of the parts to belong to the admiral, one part to the salvers, and one-third part to the proprietor of the ground on which the whales are drove ashore, and appoints two honest men to divide the whales, and mark them with the letters A. B. C. These dividers are judicially sworn to divide them equally, which being done, each third share is marked with a letter, and drawn accordingly as decerned by the admiral; the minister or vicar of the parish claims the tythes of the whole,
and

and commonly gets it; the baillie also claims the heads for his attendance, and if the admiral find that he has done his duty, the heads are decerned to him, otherways not. The biggest of these whales will be about 18 or 20 foot long; but most of them not half that length; of their spih they make oil, and the best kind will yield about a barrel of oil each over head, or a little more; but, if they are of the smaller kind, they will yield much less; there is a vast deal of trouble and charge in making the oil right.

There are in most places of these islands plenty of shell fish, such as oysters, muscles, cockles, cullock spouts, buckies, wilks, limpets, crabs, and partans; but very few lobsters.

Product of Zetland for Export.

Commodities yearly exported are, salt well dried, cod, ling, tusk, and saith fish, some stock-fish and salted herrings, butter, fish-oil, stockings and worsted stuffs, to foreign markets; and wool, horses, and skins, coast-ways to Orkney and Scotland. For exporting the fish, butter, and oil, which is the principal product of Zetland, there used formerly ten or twelve small ships to come here annually from Hamburgh and Bremen; and these Hamburgh and Bremen merchants had their booths in the most convenient places, where they received the fish, butter, and oil, from the country people. They salted and dried the fish themselves, and staid for receiving these goods from the first of May till the last of August. They paid the proprietor of the ground a considerable rent yearly for their booths, and the use of the ground upon which they cure their fish. These foreigners did yearly import hemp, lines, hooks, tar, linen-cloth, tobacco, spirits, and beer, for the fishers, and foreign money wherewith they purchased their cargoes. But when the high duty was laid upon foreign salt, and custom-house officers sent over, and a custom-house settled at Lerwick, these foreigners could not enter, and so the inhabitants, and many of the heritors or landlords, were obliged to turn merchants and

export

export the country products to foreign markets, and had, in return there for money and such other necessaries as the country could not subsist without; but the prime cost of the fish here being very dear, and a standing price which the fishers will not alter; (viz.) 3d. each ling, 1½d. each cod, and 5 shilling sterling each barrel of herrings, considering the great fatigue and charge the poor fishermen are at, and the small quantity they catch, they cannot afford to sell them cheaper; however, such a prime cost, with the value of the salt, and cash and charges in curing them; and that foreign markets often prove very precarious, the exporters seldom make much by these goods exported; nay, when ship's freight and charges are deducted, they oftener lose than gain; but the bounty-money allowed upon fish exported helps to stop some of the charges, otherwise they could not be able to carry on that trade, as markets have been abroad for several years past, that neither fish, butter, nor oil, has given any price. Saith fish are only catched in the parish of Dunrosnes, and are cured with home salt, and sent coast-ways, and sold at Leith and Dundee; there are but few herrings cured here for export, by the inhabitants; but vast quantities are taken yearly by the Hollanders upon our coast in the months of June and July, that being the time that the herrings are best; the bounty-money allowed by the government upon herrings exported is very small, being only 2s. 8d. per barrel, which discourageth our merchants to cure them for export, being a great charge in curing them, and markets very uncertain; wool is only exported to Orkney, which is generally bartered with the Orkney men; as also our little horses, called by them shelties, for worsted stiffs, and linen cloth.

The longest days here may be reckoned about twenty hours, for from the first of May to the middle of July, we have no night, but a twilight for a few hours, so that one may read a letter at 12 o'clock at night, if the horizon be not very much overclouded; and the shortest day, which is the beginning of December, will be about 5 hours, the sun rising a little before ten, and setting as much before three.

CHAPTER

CHAPTER IV.

Of the Manners, Language, and Religion.

MANNERS.] The ancient inhabitants of Zetland were a very indolent simple sort of people, who lived very meanly : they were all fishers, and their food for the most part was fish and milk, being at little or no pains to improve the ground, so they had little bread, or malt drink. They drank a sort of whey, called *bland,* of which they made considerable quantities in summer, while they had plenty of milk, and laid it up for winter stores, and it is still the drink most used here amongst the poorer sort, who are not able to afford better ; and it is said, that the men were stronger, and lived much longer, before they knew the use of malt drink, or spirits, than what they do now since these became more cŏmmon. They had but little arable ground, and that was for the most part the property of the posses- sors thereof, who were all little heritors, or udellers, and was conveyed to their successors by a title called *Udell Suc- cession,* of which afterwards. After Zetland became sub- ject to the crown of Scotland many Scotish people came over to it, some in a civil, others in an ecclesiastic capa- city, and settled here, who in process of time acquired most of the arable land from the ancient inhabitants, who be- came their tenants, and were obliged to improve that ground for others which formerly they had neither thrift nor sense to do for themselves. These in-comers brought the customs and manners of the party they came from to take place here, and are at present much the same as in Scotland. Most people of condition having their children educated at Edinburgh, the gentry are as polite here as else- where, and live as handsome, according to their small income, and what they can afford, as any in Britain of their rank ; the common people also in their manners and way of living are no way inferior to those of that kind in the north parts of Britain; and most of them striving to live better than what they can afford, they are generally poor, but it is with them as in all other places, the industrious and saving are

rich,

rich, and the indolent and careless miserable poor; the last being still most numerous in the islands of Zetland.

LANGUAGE.] The ancient language spoken by the inhabitants of Zetland was that of the Norwegians called *Norn*, and continued to be that only spoken by the natives till of late, and many of them speak it to this day amongst themselves; but the language now spoken here is English, which they pronounce with a very good accent; and many, especially about Lerwick, speak Dutch very well, having had frequent occasion to converse with the Dutch people.

RELIGION.] The ancient religion of Zetland was Paganism; but the Christian religion was planted here as soon as in the Orkneys, they being from the beginning one bishoprick. Who was the first bishop, and how many bishops there have been of Orkney and Zetland, may be seen in our Church Histories of Scotland, to which I shall refer any who want to be informed thereof; but the bishop still had his residence in Orkney, and planted Zetland with priests and such other clergymen as he thought proper, who made it their business to instruct the poor simple inhabitants, who were naturally superstitious, in all the gross errors of the church of Rome, especially the doctrine of merit, by which they persuaded the ignorant Udellers to make donations of their lands to the church, in the name of some Saint, who would intercede for them, and bring them to heaven, as they believed; whereby a great part of the Udel lands of Zetland came to the bishop of Orkney. The first protestant bishop of Orkney and Zetland is said to have been Adam Bothwell, who, having been long bishop thereof, did at last make an exchange of that bishoprick with Robert Steuart, natural son to king James V. for the abbacy of Holy-rood-house, of which the said Robert was prior, by a gift from the king his father. This Robert Steuart having got possession of the said bishoprick, and the Sinclairs, formerly earls of Orkney, being attainted for some crime against the crown, the said Robert was by king James VI. created earl of Orkney and lord Zetland, upon the 21st day of October, 1570, the said earldom and lordship being by the king
made

made over to him and his heirs for ever, he became heritable proprietor thereof, together with the bishoprick at that time. Being shortly after the Reformation the church of Scotland was under presbyterian government, with a superintendant in each diocese, with something of episcopal power in church affairs. But whoever was superintendant of Orkney, earl Robert during his life, and Patrick his son and successor after his death, did rule in all matters civil and ecclesiastick at their pleasure. Anno 1606, the king, with consent of parliament, having established episcopal church goverment in Scotland, *James Law* was made bishop of Orkney and Zetland; but he received none of the bishop's rents as long as Patrick earl of Orkney lived, after whose death and forfeiture, the islands of Orkney and Zetland were annexed to the crown of Scotland; and the said bishop Law, with consent of his chapter, did enter into contract with the king; whereby they dispone and resign to his majesty and his royal successors all their ecclesiastical lands and possessions in Orkney and Zetland with all rights and securities belonging thereto, to be incorporate and united to the crown for ever; and the king gives back and dispones to the bishop as much lands and tythes in Orkney as his majesty judged a sufficient patrimony to the bishop of Orkney and Zetland, to be possessed and enjoyed by him and his successors in all time coming: the king also disponed to the bishop and his successors the right of patronage to present to all the vicarages of Orkney and Zetland, with power to them to present qualified ministers as often as the kirks became vacant, disponing also to them the heritable and perpetual right of jurisdiction of sheriff and bailiffe within the lands and patrimony of the bishoprick, excerning all possessors thereof in all causes, civil and criminal, from the jurisdiction of the sheriff and steward of the earldom, together also with the commissarist of Orkney and Zetland, with power to constitute and ordain commissars clerks, and other members of court. This contract betwixt the king and the bishop was made anno 1614, containing several other church privileges and benefices to ministers; which was

in

in the following year ratified and confirmed by Act of
Parliament, called the Act of Platt, whereby all the ministers of Orkney and Zetland were provided to stipends,
which continue so still.   To this Bishop Law succeeded
George Graham, anno 1615, as bishop of Orkney and Zetland, who possessed that bishoprick till anno 1638 ; at
which time the church of Scotland being again brought
under Presbyterian government, Graham was divested of
his bishoprick, and during the continuance of Presbytrie,
the bishop's rents of Orkney were granted by Parliament
to the city of Edinburgh, who uplifted them by factors and
farmers till anno 1662; that episcopasie was restored by
king Charles II. after his restoration, who made *Thomas
St. Serf* bishop of Orkney and Zetland; he lived about two
years after his instalment, and was succeeded by *Andrew
Honyman*, anno 1644, as bishop of Orkney and Zetland,
who held the said bishoprick till anno 1676. To him succeeded *Murdock Mackenzie*, who continued in the possession
of that bishoprick till anno 1688, about which time the Re-
volution happened in Scotland, and Presbyterian church
government was restored.   But the ministers of Orkney
and Zetland continued in their charges, under their episcopal ordination, without any disturbance, being never
enquired after till anno 1700, that a committee was sent
over by the general assembly to settle the church government in Orkney and Zetland, where all the ministers con-
formed to Presbytrie, and signed the confession of faith,
and were continued in their kirks, save two or three, more
bigotted than prudent, who would not conform, so were
turned out of their kirks. And ever since Zetland has been
under Presbyterian church government.   There are in Zetland twelve ministers, besides the new erection of Fair Isle
and Foully mentioned before. These thirteen ministers
make the Presbytrie of Zetland, who send yearly one of
their number as commissioner for them to the general assembly. Each of these ministers have the charge of a parish,
and in each parish in Zetland, save Lerwick, there are two,
and in some three parish churches. The country, being
most part barren mountains, is but thinly inhabited, which
makes

makes wide parishes, and finds the ministers abundance of fatigue in travelling through their charges about their ministerial work, wherein many of them are very careful, and the people, generally speaking, are most obedient and submissive to them, and the ministers here, as in other places, are esteemed and reverenced according to their prudent and becoming conversation. Their church discipline by kirk sessions, constituted of elders and deacons, is in the same manner as commonly practised in Scotland. Before the Restoration of patronage, the Presbytrie had the power of presenting ministers to vacant congregations; but, by the act restoring patronages in the reign of the late queen Anne, that of Orkney and Zetland was by her majesty bestowed upon the right honourable the earl of Morton, who is patron of all the kirks in Orkney and Zetland. This act of patronage is reckoned a great grievance by our Presbyterian ministers, and presentations are very ill looked upon by them, especially the hotter sort. However, there was never any opposition made to them here; for the earl having always treated the Presbytrie with a great deal of civility and kindness, they are most unwilling to go upon any thing that might in the least disoblige his lordship. Whenever a parish becomes vacant, the earl presents some qualified person to be minister thereof, who having past the ordinary trials, before the Presbytrie, and been approven by them, as also having a popular call from the parish where he is to be minister, he is then ordained minister in common form, by laying on of the hands of the Presbytrie, &c. While any parish remains vacant, the vacant stipend is collected by the earl's orders, which his lordship always bestows upon pious uses in the parish; and did never appropriate a farthing thereof to any other use.

There being no fund in any parish in Zetland for a school, few of the common people were taught to read. The want of parochial schools has been long much complained of by the ministers, and many efforts were made to have a school settled in every parish by a voluntary contribution of the inhabitants, which when set up in any one place in the parish was found to be of little use to the

whole

whole, they lying so discontiguous, and those at a distance were not capable to board their children from home; so such as had no benefit by the school refused to pay their quotas; and hence the school broke up before it was well settled, and we have only one school for Zetland from the Society for Propagating of Christian Knowledge, which has been in several parishes. In anno 1725 a proposal was set on foot for settling a fund in each parish for maintaining a school, and in a full meeting of the heritors at the head court the scheme was presented to them by the steward depute, copies thereof having been sent several months before to the whole baillies in the country, to be intimate to the heritors in their respective parishes; and the right honourable the earl of Morton having consented thereto, the whole heritors of Zetland did sign their consent also, and craved that an act might be made thereupon, and the authority of the Steuart court interposed thereto, which was accordingly done. The Proposal and Act thereupon is in the Appendix to this book, which now obtains in several parishes, and in others much neglected, just as the principal heritor of the parish stands inclined to promote such a public good work.

CHAPTER V.

Of the Government of ZETLAND, *ancient and modern.*

THE most ancient government that can any way be gathered of Zetland is that it was under while subject to the kings of Norway and Denmark, who had a governor here called the *Fowd* of Zetland, who was judge in all causes civil and criminal. Under him was a judge in every parish, called the *Fowd* of the parish, who only was judge in small matters, and for keeping of good neighbourhood amongst the inhabitants, and in case of anything falling out above his jurisdiction, he was to acquaint the grand Fowd thereof, and to send the malefactor to him to be tried. The Fowd of Zetland was also chamberlain, and
collected

collected the crown rent, which was at that time only a redendo called *Scat*, payable in butter, fish oil, and a sort of very coarse cloth, called *wad-mill*; the arable ground being all at first the property of the immediate possessors thereof, which went to their successors by a verbal title called *Udell succession*, whereby all the children, male and female, succeed equally to the father in his estate, heritable and moveable. These poor Udellers were miserably oppressed by the governor, or Fowd, and kept under, being forbidden all sort of commerce with foreigners, as the subjects of that king are to this day in Fairo and Island; so there was no such thing as money amongst them; and what they had of the country product more than paid the crown rent, they were obliged to bring to the governor, who gave them for it such necessaries as they could not be without, and at what prices he had a mind, wherewith they were obliged to rest content, having no way to be redressed. Kept under this slavery they were miserably poor, careless, and indolent, and most of their young men, when grown up, finding the poor living their native country was likely to afford them, went abroad, and served in foreign countries for their bread, and seldom or never returned; so that these islands were but thinly inhabited. Thus Zetland continued under the Danish government, until the year 1470, that king James the Third of Scotland was married to Margaret daughter to the king of Denmark, with whom he got the islands of Orkney and Zetland in dowry, said to be redeemable by the king of Denmark for fifty thousand florins of the Pikine, to be paid to the king of Scotland. But the king of Denmark did, upon the birth of King James the Fourth, his grandson, renounce by a charter under his great seal all right, title, and claim, which he or his successors, kings of Denmark might have, or pretend, to the islands of Orkney and Zetland for ever; reserving to his subjects the Danes their private estates in these islands, which they actually held in Zetland for many years thereafter, till they were at last purchased from them by several gentlemen in Zetland, and are known by the name of *Noraway lands* to this day. And this re-

nunciation

nunciation of these islands is again confirmed by Christian King of Denmark unto king James the Sixth, when he married the princess Anne of Denmark, sister to the said Christian.

After the islands of Orkney and Zetland became subject to the crown of Scotland, they were conferred by the king upon some noble favourite, with the dignity of earl of Orkney; amongst whom the Sinclairs, earls of Orkney, are said to be the longest possessors, but at what time, and how long, they were earls of Orkney I have seen no sufficient documents, and therefore shall refer the history of that ancient and honourable family to some better hands.

The first I find dignified with the title of Orkney, after the Sinclairs earls of Orkney, is *James Hepburn*, earl of Bothwell, who was created duke of Orkney by Mary queen of Scotland, so as he might be the more honourable match for her majesty, who was married to him upon the 15th of May, 1567, in the palace of Holy-rood-house, by Adam Bothwell, bishop of Orkney. This James Duke of Orkney built the castle of Noutland in Westera, a small island in Orkney. He is said to be no good man; and being hated by the nobility, as suspected to have an active hand in the murther of Henry lord Darnly, the queen's former husband, he was forced to fly for his life, and came to Orkney, where he found but cold entertainment. From that he came to Zetland, where having staid some time, he went to Noraway, where he was taken prisoner by order of the king of Denmark, and carried to Copenhagen, where he died, after having lain ten years in a vile prison. Thus ended James duke of Orkney, who had as little pleasure in his high dignity, as Orkney had credit by his bearing the title thereof.

Robert Stewart, natural son to king James the Fifth, by Euphara, daughter to Alexander lord Elphingston, was created earl of Orkney and lord Zetland, by king James the Sixth, upon the 21st day of October, 1570. This Robert being formerly prior of Holy Rood house, which he exchanged with Adam Bothwell bishop of Orkney for that bishoprick, as mentioned before; he took possession not

only

only of the earldom of Orkney, and lordship of Zetland, but also of the bishop's rents thereof, and so became sole proprietor of the crown rents, and that of the bishoprick; the last whereof was become very considerable, under the management of the popish clergy, unto which he added new acquisitions of lands made by himself, as purchased from the Udellers, more by oppression and forfeitures than for payment of the value, as is reported of him; and also that he exercised a very arbitrary and tyrannical government over his dominions of Orkney and Zetland, all affairs sacred and civil therein being ordered according to his good will and pleasure. He lived sometimes in Zetland, and built a house at Samburgh, in the parish of Dunrosness, the ruins whereof are yet standing, called the *Westhouse*. He had also a house at Wethersta, in the parish of Delting, as appears by his few charter granted to Andrew Gifford, of Wethersta, dated the 8th day of July, 1583, wherein he reserves for his own use two or three rooms in the house of Wethersta. This Robert earl of Orkney was married to Jean daughter to the earl of Cassell, by whom he had Patrick his son and successor.

Patrick, earl of Orkney and Lord of Zetland, after his father's death came to the possession of these islands, and began his government in the same manner his father ruled before him; but is said to be much more vicious and oppressive than his predecessor. Spotswood gives a character of him in these words: " This nobleman (says he) hav-
" ing undone his estate by riotous prodigality, did seek
" by unlawful shifts to repair the same, making unjust
" acts in his courts, and exacting penalties for the breach
" thereof: if any man was tried, to have concealed any-
" thing that might infer a pecuniary mulct, and bring pro-
" fit to the earl, his lands and goods were declared con-
" fiscated; or, if any person did sue for justice before any
" other judge than his deputies, his goods were escheated,
" or if they went forth of the isles without his licence, or
" his deputes, upon whatsoever occasion, they should
" forfeit their moveables, and which of all his acts
" were most inhumane, he ordered, if any man was tried
" to

" to supply, or give relief unto ships, or any vessels dis-
" tressed by tempest, the same should be punished in his
" person, and fined at the earl's pleasure."

These acts of the earl's being complained of, and he himself confessing them before the council, they were by them
declared unlawful, and the execution of them prohibited
in all time coming. And the king being frequently impor-
tuned by complaints from the poor oppressed inhabitants
of Orkney and Zetland, his majesty was pleased to resolve
upon redeeming them from the tyranny they had long
groaned under, and for effectuating thereof did purchase
from Sir John Arnut a mortgage that he had from Patrick
earl of Orkney, upon Orkney and Zetland, in anno 1613,
and thereby the king, having taken these islands into his
own hands, sent Sir James Steuart, lord Ochiltree to take
possession thereof, as his majesty's chamberlain, and
stewart of Orkney and Zetland, which earl Patrick,
then a prisoner in Dumbarton castle, opposed, by sending
Robert Stewart, his bastard son, with express command to
oppose the king's taking possession of these islands. This
he did, but was over-powered by the king's party and
carried prisoner, with several more of the earl's servants,
to Edinburgh, where they were all hanged at the cross.
And in 1614 earl Patrick was brought from Dumbarton to
Edinburgh, where he was tried upon several crimes of
treason and oppression, libelled against him, wherein he
was found guilty, and condemned to be executed, and
accordingly was beheaded on the 6th day of February
said year, and his estate forefault to the crown. This
Patrick earl of Orkney built the castle of Scallaway, mentioned before. He had by oppression, purchased a great
deal of lands from the poor Udellers of Zetland; which acquisitions made by him and his father, together with
several annual payments imposed by them upon the poor
inhabitants, had raised the crown rents of Zetland to
double what they formerly paid to any of their predecessors. And so ended the family of Steuarts earls of Orkney
and lords of Zetland.

The king being thus peaceably possessed of these
islands

islands of Orkney and Zetland, they were annexed to the crown by act of parliament, and erected into a steuartrie, and an exact rental made out of the whole rents as paid unto Patrick earl of Orkney; which rental is recorded in the court of exchequer: and these rents were thereafter paid in yearly to the king's exchequer by chamberlains and taxmen, until anno 1647, that a wadset or mortgage of these islands of Orkney and Zetland was made over by king Charles I. unto the right honourable *William Douglas* earl of *Morton*, lord high treasurer of Scotland, and knight of the garter, together with the jurisdiction thereof. To him succeeded his son *Robert* earl of Morton; who was succeeded by his son *William* earl of Morton, who continued in the possession of Orkney and Zetland until anno 1662: that king Charles the Second was pleased to redeem the earl of Morton's right to those islands of Orkney and Zetland, and they were again annexed to the crown by act of parliament, parliament IId. of Charles II. Sessions I. c. 13, and erected into a steuartrie, not to be again dissolved from the crown without consent of parliament.

Orkney and Zetland being thus again annexed to the crown, the king was pleased to make a grant of the rents thereof, together with the jurisdiction, unto *George* viscount of *Grandison*, under the conduct and management of John earl of Middletown, William duke of Hamilton, William earl of Morton, and Sir Andrew Ramsay of Abotshill, with full power granted unto them by the king, not only to set long tacks, and heritable fews, of the king's property lands, but also to grant charters to the heritors and udellers upon their udel lands, holding few of the crown for payment of an annual reddendo, formerly paid, called the *Scat* and *Watle*, and for that end they sent over Alexander Douglas, of Spynic, their deputy, clothed with a full power and commission to set long tacks, and heritable fews of the king's property lands in Zetland and Orkney for payment of a certain few duty yearly; and also to grant charters to the heritors and udellers upon their udel lands, holding in few of the king as superior for the annual payment of a reddendo, called the Scat and Watle.

So

So all the heritors and fewers in Orkney and Zetland did take holdings from Spynic, as having full power in the manner above-mentioned for granting thereof, excepting such of the heritors as had formerly got charters of Confirmation from the crown, of which there was only in Zetland Sinclair of Brough. By granting of these charters, Spynic raised a very considerable sum of money of the heritors and fewers of Orkney and Zetland, as appears by a particular account thereof for Zetland, amounting to the sum of 15,000 pounds Scots, which was very heavy upon many of them. This Alexander Douglas of Spynic continued steuart-depute and chamberlain of the crown-rents of Orkney and Zetland, until anno 1669, that the king was pleased to recall the grant made to the viscount of Grandison, and the act of annexation of the islands of Orkney and Zetland to the crown was again ratified by parliament, and the rents thereof were yearly paid in to the court of exchequer by the taxmen and chamberlains of the same, as following :

Anno 1670, Mr. George Scot, of Giblistown, was made steuart of Orkney and Zetland, and taxman of the crown rents thereof, payable to the king's exchequer. He continued five years.

Anno 1675, captain Andrew Dick was made steuart of Orkney and Zetland, and taxman of the crown-rents thereof, accountable to the court of exchequer, who continued five years.

Anno 1681, Charles Murray, of Hadon, and Sir Robert Milne, of Barntown, became taxmen and steuarts of Orkney and Zetland, accomptable to the exchequer, and continued five years.

Anno 1686, William Craige, of Garsay, was made steuart of Orkney and Zetland, and taxman of the crown-rents thereof, payable to the exchequer, which he kept five years.

Anno 1691, Colonel Robert Elphingston, of Lapness, was made steuart and chamberlain of Orkney and Zetland, accomptable to the exchequer. He continued two years.

Anno 1693, Sir Alexander Brand, of Brandsfield, became
steuart

steuart and taxman of the rents of Orkney and Zetland, payable to the exchequer, and continued four years.

Anno 1697, the honourable Mr. Robert Douglass, afterward earl of Morton, was made steuart and taxman of the crown-rents of Orkney and Zetland, and continued one year.

Anno 1698, Sir William Menzie, and Sir Samuel Maclallen, became steuarts and taxmen of the crown-rents of these islands, accountable to the exchequer, and continued five years.

Anno 1703, the right honourable James Douglass, earl of Morton, got the crown-rents of Orkney and Zetland, together with the jurisdictions thereof, from queen Anne, he being accountable to her majesty's exchequer for these rents; but the queen having taken into consideration the great loss and damage that the ancient and honourable family of Morton had sustained by their constant and firm adherence to the interest of the royal family, especially during the civil wars, in the reign of king Charles I. and Cromwell's usurpation, whereby that once eminent and illustrious family of Morton was brought very low; her majesty was pleased by her gift and disposition, dated at her court at Kensington, upon the first day of February, anno 1706-7, to dissolve from the crown, and dispone unto James earl of Morton, his heirs and successors, the earldom of Orkney and lordship of Zetland, with a charter thereupon, under the great seal, ratified and confirmed by consent of parliament. The said noble earl holding the said earldom and lordship in few of the crown for the yearly payment of the sum of 500 pounds sterling money, in name of few duty, the said earldom and lordship being redeemable by the crown for payment to the said noble earl, his heirs or successor, of the sum of 30,000 pounds sterling. By this gift and disposition, the earl of Morton is heritable steuart, justiciary, sheriff, and bailliff, within the earldom of Orkney and lordship of Zetland, and is judge competent in all causes, civil and criminal, within that jurisdiction, excepting high-treason, reductions, improbations, redemptions, and suspensions, having all the powers competent to a lord of regality in Scotland, excepting that power which they have of directing

directing of briefs, and serving them before themselves; but all briefs of land in the steuartrie are raised from the court of chancery, and retoured thereto. The earl of Morton has also power by his gift from the crown to grant charters of confirmation to the heritors and fewers of Orkney and Zetland to hold of the crown for payment of the usual few duty; the said noble earl by his said gift is also patron of all the kirks in Orkney and Zetland.

The earl of Morton, as heritable steuart and justiciar of Orkney and Zetland, appoints and commissions deputes there for administering of justice to the lieges, and punishing of malefactors, conform to the laws and practice of Scotland. The steuart deputes, keeps, and holds courts as often as there is occasion for them; but he has two head courts in the year, one in the beginning of November, the other in the beginning of June, at which the whole heritors and fewers are obliged by their holdings to compear, being duly advertised thereof by the steuart clerk, or the baillie of the parish where they live; and being called in the court three several days, and not compearing, nor any reason offered, for their not compearance, the absents are fined, each, in 40l. Scots money. The steuart clerk has his commission from the earl as steuart principal; not but the steuart depute can employ his own clerk upon occasion, as he doth all other members of court needful; but the steuart clerk only should record all court processes, and give out extracts. The steuart depute is also obliged to hold circuit courts in each parish once a year; but the steuart depute of Zetland having no salary, save the emoluments of the court, which is seldom so much as pays the necessary members thereof, he cannot afford to be at the charge of travelling through the country, with such a retinue as all the members of the court make out; it being very expensive travelling through this country, and therefore these circuit courts are much laid aside.

There is also a bailliff in each parish, who holds his commission either of the steuart principal, or his depute, having power to hold courts within his bailliffrie, to make his own clerk, and other court members needful, and is judge

in

in small matters, such as keeping good neighbourhood; but can decern in no cause above 10*l.* Scots value, unless otherwise provided by his commission.   The bailliff is obliged to keep a court-book, wherein all causes brought before his court are recorded; and that book must be produced to the steuart depute when called for at his circuit courts.   If the book is regularly kept, and nothing amiss in it, then it is approven; if otherwise, the bailiff is enjoined by the stewart depute to amend what is amiss, or to lose his commission.   Under the baillie there are ten or twelve honest men of the parish called *Rancelmen.* These are judicially appointed and chosen in the bailliff court : the whole householders of the parish being present are asked, if they have any thing to object against such a man, why he should not be made a Rancelman; and no objection being made, he is entered into that office, and takes an oath to be faithful and diligent therein, and the Rancelman's instructions and power being read in open court, and recorded in the court-book, each Rancelman may have an extract thereof, if he please.   These instructions are in the Appendix.   The Rancelman has the power of a constable, to command the inhabitants to keep the peace, and to call for assistance; and to enter any house within the parish at all hours of the day or night, and search the house for stolen goods, which they call *ranciling*; and if they find any thing that the owner of the house cannot give a good account how he came by it, then they seize him directly, and carry him to the bailliff, who takes precognition of the cause; and if it infers the crime of theft, then the thief, with the *fang* or thing stolen found in his custody, is sent to the prison, and the steuart depute acquainted thereof, who appoints a day for trying the thief according to law, and in case the bailliff finds that the representation of the rancelman will not amount to any proof of the crime of theft, he dismisseth the suspected thief, upon his good behaviour, with certification.   There are in Zetland a great many municipal laws called *country acts*, and these municipal laws are the rule that the baillifs chiefly act by. These country acts are in the Appendix, and are or should

be

be read over twice in the year, at the bailliff-courts, when all the householders are present, at which two courts, being Martinmas and Whitsunday courts, if any householder is wilfully absent, the bailliff fines the absent in forty shillings Scots each time they are absent, and can give no good reason for their absence. The rancelmen are to give up lists of the poor in the parish at the bailliff-court; and they are appointed to be quartered on the parish for maintenance, and money is ordered them by the kirk session, out of the poor's-box, for buying of cloaths; so there are no beggars allowed to go from parish to parish, nor from house to house, otherways than they are appointed; and if they can work any thing, they are put to it in the houses where they are lodged. In some parishes of the country, these rancelmen, and other intelligent honest men of the parish, are erected of late into a society, for reformation of manners and regulating of servants, Zetland being very much straitened for want of servants, masters for the most part being so poor, that they can give servants little encouragement; the instructions to which society are in the Appendix. There is also in each parish a *law-right man*, that is, an honest man, appointed judicially by the bailliff, as the rancelmen are. His business is to weigh and measure the rent-butter and oil; and also to judge of the quality thereof, and, if he finds it insufficient, to return it as not receivable. He is sworn to do justice, and keep just weights and measures.

The right honourable the earl of Morton is at present high admiral of Scotland, and was before vice-admiral of Orkney and Zetland, and appoints his deputes there, who have by their commission all the powers and privileges provided by the laws of Scotland to that judicatory, in all maritime affairs, of which there is little that falls under the cognizance of the admiral of Zetland, save that of wrecks, which sometimes happen, and in that particular the admiral of Zetland, as there in most other places, is more under the direction of the country practice, than any statuary laws; but the practice here is still so much controverted, that it is very difficult to find such precedents as

can

can stand for a rule therein. However I shall give a short specimen of the most common and least controverted practice that has prevailed in Zetland for some time past, relating to wrecks or stranded ships ; that is, whenever a ship is forced ashore by bad weather, or otherways, and seems to be irrecoverable, the baillie of the parish, or proprietor of the ground where the wreck happens, does immediately acquaint the admiral depute thereof, who forthwith repairs to that place with his clerk and other court members ; and if the master, or any person belonging to the ship, is saved alive, he is allowed to put in a petition to the admiral, craving that the ship may be declared wreck, and that he may give orders for salving, and securing all the wrecked goods that can be salved, for behoof of the true owner or proprietor thereof; which petition being considered by the admiral, having called an admiral court upon the place where the wreck is, and finding the ship irrecoverable, declares her wreck, and ordains the best anchor or cable, or value thereof, to belong to the phiscal of court for his majesty's interest, and appoints salvers for saving the whole wreck as far as possible, and securing the same for a reasonable salvage, to be decerned according to the trouble and charge in saving thereof, and the value of the subject salved according to justice; and if the petitioner can instruct his title to the ship and cargo wrecked, by a vendition or other sufficient vouchers, the admiral decerns the whole subject saved, excepting the best anchor and cable to belong to him upon payment of a reasonable salvage, and the charges of the court ; and in case the petitioner cannot instruct his title to the ship and cargo, the admiral ordains the whole wreck salved to belong to the phiscal of the court for the king's interest, and his majesty's donators, or to the true proprietor, instructing his title thereto within term of law ; and when all is salved, there is a just inventory thereof given up by the salvers upon oath ; and the principal salver is ordained to deliver up the whole subject salved, conform to said inventory, upon payment of in name of salvage, together with the best anchor and cable, to be delivered

livered to the phiscal, with the sum of
as the necessary charges of the court. And if any person
or persons shall intromet with any part of the wreck, without order from the admiral, or those employed by him as
salvers, they are sued at the instance of the phiscal as im-
bezlers, and ordained to deliver what they intromitted
with, and fined for their vitious and irregular intromissions;
and the principal salver is obliged to secure all the wreck
goods salved until carried off, or disposed upon by the proprietor.

And thus there is no place in the world where ship-
wreckt men are better used, nor the proprietors' interest
more cared for than in Zetland.

The proprietor of the ground where the wreck falls always
claims a share of the wreck, pleading the old country practice, which was that all wrecks were divided into three
shares, one thereof to the proprietor of the ground, one to the
salver, and the other to the proprietor, if any appeared, which
failing, to the king, with the best anchor and cable to the
admiral. But the admiral court for several years past has
not followed that practice, being thought exorbitant, and
only allows the heritor any damage his ground may sus-
tain, and some allowance for the use of it; which is thought
by many a great hardship upon the heritors, and a cutting
them out of their ancient privilege. But for preventing
of any clamours of that kind, the admiral does, and always
should, make the proprietor of the ground the principal
salver, and beside reasonable salvage ordain him a premium
for the use of his ground and personal trouble, wherewith
every reasonable man is satisfied.

If the wreck happens to be a direlict, and no person
appears to claim it, the phiscal of the court puts in a
petition to the admiral, holding forth the state of the wreck,
craving, that in regard there is no living person to claim
the wreck, it may be declared an absolute wreck and
direlict, and decerned to belong to the king and his majesty's
donators, or to the true owner or proprietor, instructing
his title within term of law, and that salvers may be
appointed. The admiral being fully satisfied anent the
truth

truth of the petition, decerns according thereunto, and appoints the proprietor of the ground where the wreck is to be principal salver, with power to employ as many salvers as is needful, who are all obliged to give up an account, upon oath, to the admiral, of what they saved; and are paid a reasonable salvage according to the trouble and charge they have been at, of which accounts are given in, and the proprietor of the ground is allowed a permium as above. And in case the wreck goods saved are in a perishing condition, and cannot be preserved, then the admiral orders public intimation to be made to the whole country by placarts put up in the most public places, intimating, that upon such a day, and place, such a parcel of wreck goods is to be sold by way of public roup, to the highest bidder, with the conditions of the roup; and the money is lodged in the clerk's hands; the court being answerable therefore to any having right to the same. I have formerly mentioned the country practice anent small whales driven ashore and killed by the country people, that is, they are equally divided into three shares; one thereof to the admiral, one to the salvers, and one to the proprietor of the ground upon which they are driven ashore; and that practice still obtains without any alteration; and the minister or vicar of the parish claims the tythes of them, which has been much controverted, because all the boats employed in driving these whales pay a compound tythe to the vicar yearly, so much for each boat; and the catching of these whales being a part of their fishing, it is thought the vicar has no more title to the tythes of the whales, than he has to the tythe of the cod and ling they catch after the composition; and that he may as justly demand the one as the other. However, it commonly obtains; the minister of the parish being in most parishes vicar, he sticks close by it, and they are unwilling to contend with him. The Admiral still claims all derelicts cast in by the sea, and if of any value, still gets it upon the above footing of payment of salvage, and a premium to the proprietor of the ground it falls upon. But there is a sort of wreck called by the country people *ragha*,
that

that is pieces of fir-wood, which has never been in any use, and is thought to drive from the north ports of Norway and America, of which there used long ago great quantities to drive about the country; but for many years past very little of that kind has been found. This sort of wreck the inhabitants have still thought the unquestionable property of the finder thereof, and they use it for repairing their houses, and should the admiral enquire after it, he could make nothing of it, and therefore it has not been noticed hitherto. The timber brought here from Norway is very dear, and the poor inhabitants are not able to buy it. So many of them depend upon that wreck timber, which they call *godsend*, and still think they have a better title to it, than any else have, and therewith they repair their small houses.

There is here also a commissary, who is judge in all consistorial affairs. We have also justices of the peace, and commissioners of supply for imposing the land-tax.

In the town of Lerwick there is a custom-house, where all ships coming to the country and going out of it in the way of trade make entries, take out clearances, and pay the king's duty, as in any other part in Scotland, there being therein all the proper offices, such as a collector, a comptroller, surveyor, land-waiter, and searcher, with tide-waiters, who give constant attendance for dispatches; but they have very little business, and were it not for seeing foreign salt imported, and the fish cured therewith exported, they would have no business at all. The country is very poor, and no manner of consumption for goods to be imported that pay duty, and therefore there is little or nothing imported, save some trifles for carrying on the fishing trade, by which only the inhabitants chiefly subsist.

There have been excise-officers here also, but finding little or no business, they were removed; and for several years past the excise of Zetland has been farmed by a gentleman of this country, for about 40 or 50 pounds a year, and I am well assured he makes little by it, because there is not one brewer, nor a tanner, nor a tallow-chandler in Zetland. The few retailers of ale here brew the ale they re-

tail

tail themselves. The malt for the most part used here comes from Orkney and Scotland ; as do also the leather and shoes used here for the most part. Most of the leather and skins tanned here is by the poor fishermen for cloaths, and that mostly with the roots of tormentil, instead of bark, and the paying the leather duty for that is a very great hardship upon the poor people, and I am persuaded was never designed by the legislator. There are no candles sold here, and the few that are used are made by those that use them. There is very little malt made in Zetland, they having no corn to make it of; and I have all the reason in the world to believe, that, were the government rightly informed anent the exciseables of Zetland, they would see it not worth while to be enquired after.

CHAPTER VI.

Of the ancient and modern way of transmiting property in ZETLAND.

THE most ancient way how lands and heritage was transmitted to property was by a verbal deed called *Udell succession,* founded upon an old Norwegian law, called *St. Olla's law,* by which a man could no way dispose of or burden the lands he had by his father ; neither had he any power to make a will contrary to the said law ; but whatever children he had, male or female, they all succeeded equally to the father in his estate, heritable and moveable, and the youngest son had the father's dwelling-house, because the elder children were commonly *foris familiat* before the father's death, and the youngest son staid with him, and supported him in his old age, and thereby had no opportunity to provide himself in a settlement, and therefore was provided with his father's dwelling-house, which was also an inducement to make him more careful of his old father. By this way of succession most of the inhabitants were proprietors of the lands they possessed, and very few tenants amongst them ; and this Udell
succession

succession continued with many of the small Udellers of Zetland, till the year 1664, that they took heritable tacks of their own udel lands from Spynic.

The first rights that are to be found upon lands in Zetland is that called a *Shaynd Bill*, and that only used by the most considerable heritors. *Shynd* in the Danish language signifies a *court*, and *Bill* was a common name to any deed or writing made in court; so it may be rendered in English, a judicial right. The way how it was done was thus : A man having a mind to dispone his estate, invited the Fowd and 3 or 4 of the best men in the country to his house, where he had an entertainment provided for them, and being all convened, the Fowd kept a court, before which the heritor compeared, and did there judicially make his will, disponing his estate heritable and moveable particularly mentioned, and divided to his children, reserving his own life-rent of the whole, and a life-rent of a part to his wife, if she survived him, which will the clerk of court wrote, and being done was publicly read, all parties concerned being present, and if approven by the disponer, it was signed by the Fowd and these 3 or 4 gentlemen that sat with him as assessors, and all their seals were put to it, and being recorded in the court books, the principal was delivered to the disponer, who kept it till his death, and then all the heirs mentioned in the Shynd Bill entered to their respective portions contained therein, and were all equally chargeable for the defunct's debts and funeral charges. And if there was no such will made by the Udeller in his life-time, after his death his children, or nearest of kin if he had no children, made application to the Fowd to divide the inheritance amongst them, who appointed a day and place, ordaining all concerned to attend; and having called a court, he caused the heirs to give up a faithful inventory, upon oath, of the whole subject left by the heritor deceased, which he divided equally amongst them, according to the Udell or St. Olla's law, and caused a Shynd bill to be written thereupon, which was signed, sealed, and delivered to the heirs, and was as good as if made by the Udeller while he lived.

If

If any man was to make a purchase of land from an Udeller, with consent of his heirs, without which the purchase was not good, the property was conveyed to the purchaser by a Shynd bill, in the same manner as abovementioned, with this addition, that the disponer did judicially acknowledge, that he had received the full value of the land disponed, and desired that his propertie therein might instantly be transferred to the purchaser, and his heirs; and the apparent heirs of the disponer being also present, consented to the sale; and the Shynd bill being signed and sealed, was delivered by the Fowd to the disponer, who did judicially deliver it to the purchaser, with a benediction.

This Shynd bill was all the right necessary for securing any person in their property during the Danish government, and was continued as the only security upon lands in Zetland for many years after it was subject to the crown of Scotland, and it would have been very much the interest of Zetland, that no writing had ever been used in it, for the securing and transmitting of property, but being a more fair, better, and easier security than all the endless writing and long conveyances that now prevail. But when gentlemen from Scotland came to settle in Zetland, and found most of the arable ground therein parcelled out amongst the poor ancient inhabitants, by their Udell succession formerly described, excepting the lands purchased by the clergy, and brought into the bishop, and some small estates belonging to gentlemen in Norway, or Denmark, mentioned before, these incomers found no great difficulty in purchasing of land from the poor simple inhabitants, especially these having some authority, as most of them had who came to settle here, and made estates, and whether their purchases were not always such as could admit of a judicial confirmation, or if they wanted to introduce the Scots laws and customs, or partly both, I know not; but they began to lay aside the Shynd bill, and to use dispositions and sasines, and thereupon followed that long train of conveyances, filled with all the clauses and quirks that the lawyer and noter could invent, for lengthening the writ-

4   ing

ing, and making it so intricate that the true sense and
meaning thereof might only be known to themselves; so
that it came to pass, in a short process of time, that, instead of the honest, easy, and simple Shynd bill, Zetland
was stocked with rights and conveyances upon the lands,
sufficient to find the lawyers and noters as much business
as any place of its value in Scotland, whereby the ancient
simple Udellers were turned out of their old inheritances,
and obliged to improve that ground for others that they
had foolishly neglected to do for themselves.

But the heritors of Zetland being acquainted by the
gentlemen of the long robe that all their private dispositions and sasines upon their lands were only base infeftments, and so no good title, and therefore they must take
charters holding of the crown, and public infeftments
thereupon, otherways they could not maintain their property, and being thus alarmed, a favourable opportunity
presented for that purpose.   In anno 1664, Alexander
Douglas of Spynie came over with a full power and commission from the king, for receiving of resignations, and
granting charters to the heritors holding their lands in few
of the crown as noticed before; so all the heritors of Zetland
who had formerly not taken confirmations did take charters
from Spynie upon their lands. But the composition money
paid for the charters, and the great few duties payable
yearly out of the lands, did in a short time thereafter sink
many of the heritors so far in debt, that they were obliged
to sell the lands for payment thereof; for indeed the trifling
land estates of Zetland, and the very inconsiderable value
of the lands, together with the great few duties paid yearly
out of them, renders the heritors of Zetland utterly incapable of being at the charge of these public securities and
frequent confirmations required by law, as is practised in
other places, where the subject is capable of bearing the
charge, which Zetland is not, for the causes foresaid, and
therefore has been laid aside since the granting of Spynie's
charters.

The late noble and worthy Robert earl of Morton, who
knew the affairs of Zetland perfectly well, and was a very
judicious

judicious thinking nobleman, finding that the great diminution of the crown rents of Zetland, yearly payable to his
lordship, was chiefly owing to the old country practice in
these two following particulars ; as first, that the chamberlain of these rents is obliged to call for, and receive the
rents and few duties payable yearly out of the heritors
lands from every individual tenant thereof, and that in
butter, oil, and money, which occasions a vast deal of
trouble and expence to him in travelling at least once a
year through the whole country, receiving the butter and
oil, all in small parcels, packing and transporting thereof
to ports for export, and having an account to keep with
every land labourer within the country of Zetland, and
many of them proving insolvent, and the heritor of the
land no way answerable for the tenant's deficiency, which
make yearly a considerable discount of the crown rents.

2d, When the Udel or fewd lands are ley, *i.e.* not laboured,
nor a tenant upon them, these ley lands pay no scat-watle,
nor corn-tythe, although a rental tythe ; so the chamberlain
gets those ley lands yearly attested by the bailliff of each
parish, which he takes credit for in his accompts. For preventing of which two great inconveniencies to the crown-
rents, the said noble earl offered to give all the heritors of
Zetland heritable charters upon their lands, holding, as Spynie's charters do, few of the crown gratis, free of any charge,
providing they would for the future pay the few duties
yearly, without any discount, ley or laboured, as contained
in the few charter. But that the heritors would not go
into, choosing rather to stick by their ancient use of payment, that is, when the land is laboured, the labourer
thereof to be charged with the superior duty, and when by
the heritor was not chargeable with the scat, watle, and
corn-tiend, but the few duties of the fewed crown lands, is
yearly paid, whether the land is ley or laboured, but
whereby it pays no scat, nor corn-teind ; so all the lands of
Zetland stand upon the former footing, and the ley scat is
still a controverted point. The earl of Morton, as having
right to the crown rents of Zetland, pleads that the heritors
of Zetland holding their lands in few of the crown, the scat

is

is the annual reddendo, or few duty, the punctual payment whereof is the common alternative upon which all few charters subsist, and in case of non-payment of the reddendo, the few falls. Whereunto it is answered by the heritors, that by Spynie's charter they are only obliged to pay the scat-watle, &c. conform to the rental and former use of payment thereof, which is when the land is laboured the labourer is chargeable with the crown-rent, but the heritor no way chargeable therewith, ley or laboured, unless he labour it himself, and the chamberlain is left to find the labourers, or lose the crown rent; and this has been the use and custom of payment in Zetland past the memory of man. To which it was replyed by the earl, that these words *used* and *wont* import no more in any charter in Scotland than the places, terms and species, *used* and *wont*, and not any diminution of the reddendo, and that it is unreasonable to suppose, that there should be a power left in the hands of the fewer to pay the few duty, or not, as he pleased, which he may do by casting the lands ley, or labouring them, as he had a mind, and thereby rendering the crown rent most precarious and uncertain: whereunto it is again answered by the heritors, that whatever these words, *used* and *wont*, may import in any charter in Scotland, yet in the charters granted by Spynie to them, the words *used* and *wont* imply the use of payment, as well as the places and terms of payment, and rather the former, because the term of payment is mentioned in the charter, but not the particular reddendo payable, but is only said conform to the rental, and use of payment; and further, that what they assert has been the common use of payment always is evident, because it is certain the ley scat has never been paid, nor the heritor ever charged therewith, since the granting of Spynie charters, which is now 70 years, nor ever can be for granting of these charters, that can be made appear, and it is not presumable, that any man would act such a foolish part, as wilfully to lose four shillings of his own, on purpose that another should lose sixpence, which would be the case, should the heritors cast their land ley, that the crown rent might not be paid.

These

These are the principal arguments on both sides of the question, which were never yet determined ; and the heritors are still of opinion, that the constant and long continued use of payment, is sufficient to support their cause. But, whatever may be in that, I am persuaded that an accommodation of that affair betwixt the earl of Morton and the heritors of Zetland, might very much tend to the interest of both, and I believe some of the most considerable and judicious heritors would go into the foresaid proposals made by the late noble earl, with little alteration, providing the butter and oil were kept at the standard price they were at when Spynie's charters were granted, which were four shillings the *lispund* of butter, and sixpence the *can* of oil, which is more than those commodities have yielded at any market for several years bygone. The price now charged upon the heritors and fewers for the crown-rent butter, in case they fail in payment of the butter, is 4s. 10d. per lispund. The way how that price was introduced for the butter in Zetland is this; the Hamburghers and Bremeners trading here always bought the butter at a rixdollar the lispund; now a rixdollar at the time of granting Spynie's charters was only four shillings of our money, or forty-eight shillings Scots, and continued so for several years thereafter, and then that foreign coin was raised to four shillings and ten pence per dollar, at which rate it stood for many years, and was at last brought down to four shillings, or four shillings and two pence, at which it still continues ; but the butter stands at four shillings and ten pence, which is unreasonable, when the price of it abroad is less than ever formerly. The oil also came to rise the same way, from six pence to one shilling the can ; by giving a good price some years, and then falling again below that value, makes the tenants take care to pay it up in kind, which is a loss to the rents ; whereas, were the butter and oil brought to the old standard, the rents would be far more effectually paid, and consequently would be more for the earl's interest.

CHAPTER

CHAPTER VII.

Of the several Denominations of the Crown rent of
Zetland; *their original, and how paid.*

THE first and only rent paid to the crown out of the
lands of Zetland, was that called the *Scat.* The whole
island being divided into parishes, each parish is again
subdivided into *scatalds,* marked out by *march stones* and
meithes, dividing the scatalds from each other. This scatald is the pasture ground belonging to the arable land adjacent thereto, called a *room* or *town,* the name whereof is
written in the rental, with the scat yearly payable thereout
in butter, fish, oil, and a sort of very coarse cloth called
wadmill, marked in the old rentals, *lispound* and *marks*
of butter, *shillings* and *cuttels* of wadmill, and *butts* and
cans of oil. A lispound is 28 lbs weight, and in each lispound is 24 marks; a shilling of wadmill is 6 cuttals or
curtele, i.e. shortell, a measure containing 24 *canches* in
length; a butt of oil is 4 cans, each a Scots quart, and
about a mutchkin more, on account of the oil sticking by
the vessel. The wadmill rent being converted to money,
the cuttel is a groat, six whereof being a shilling, as marked
in the rental, that is a Zealand *zullen,* which is 24 shillings
Scots, or two shillings. The term of payment of the scat
is Martinmas in the subsequent year. The scat, as I said
before, was the only land rent payable to the crown out of
Zetland at first, but in process of time some of the arable
land, which was at first the property of the improver,
came also to the crown by forfeitures and donations; however, there seems to be very little of that kind before
Robert Stewart earl of Orkney came to be proprietor
thereof; for before his accession thereto, it is said the
crown rent of Zetland was farmed at 500 marks Scots a
year; but after the forfeiture of Patrick earl of Orkney,
the whole acquisition made by him and his father fell to
the crown, together with all the lands and tythes belonging
to the bishoprick, of all which, with the impositions laid
upon

upon the country by the said earls of Orkney, there was a rental made out, which rental is recorded in the king's court of exchequer, called the exchequer rental, and is the standard of the crown rents of Zetland still; at which time also king James the Sixth having transacted with James Law, bishop of Orkney, as noticed before, he gave him lands in Orkney, equivalent to the bishop's rents of Zetland; since which time the bishop of Orkney and Zetland has had no rents paid him out of Zetland; by all which means the crown rents of Zetland became very considerable in respect of what it was before those wicked men Robert and Patrick, earls of Orkney, had by oppression and arbitrary power raised these rents to such a height upon the ruin of many of the poor inhabitants, and perpetual burden of the present heritors.

2d. Species of crown rent is *land meals*, that is, the rents payable out of the crown lands, of which there are two sorts; as first, those called *property lands*, which are set by the chamberlain to tenants, who pay him the rent thereof, conform to the rental, and when ley, it pays no rent; the 2d is that part of the crown lands fewed out by Spynie, the few duties whereof the fewer is obliged to pay yearly; whether the land is ley or laboured, the rent of both is paid in butter and wadmill, as particularly set down in the rental; the butter payable at Lammas, and the wadmill at Martinmass, in the subsequent year.

3d. Species of rent is that called *Grassums*, introduced thus. When the chamberlain set a tack or lease of the property lands to a tenant he caused him to pay a grassum, or entry, the tack being commonly for 3 years: the tenant paid of grassum upon receiving the tack, two shillings for each mark land, and when the three years were out, if he had a mind to continue, the tack was again renewed for three years for payment of the like grassum; but in process of time the tenant not paying the grassum at his entry to the land, it came to be an annual payment of eight shillings Scots upon the mark land. This grassum is all the profit that the fewer of the crown lands has, the few duty being the full butter and wadmill rent contained in the

the rental; but the best of the crown lands being fewed, little of the property lands now pays grassums, being bad, and much of it still ley, and some of it set for half the rent.

4th. Is that rent called *Umboth duty*, that is the bishop's rents of Zetland, for which, as formerly observed, the bishop has the equivalent rent in Orkney. These rents are half of the corn tythes of each parish in Zetland, excepting the united parishes of Tingwall, Whitness, and Wisdale, which was an archdenrie, as noticed before. There are also in each parish some lands belonging to these Umboths, called *Bishops lands*, or *Umboth lands*. The Umboth tythes are for the most part a rental tythe, payable in butter and oil, and in some places money, or the *ipso corpore*. *Umboth* is a Danish word signifying to *change about*; the reason of which name is, that the bishop having the one half of the corn tythe of the parish, and the priest or minister of the parish the other half, the bishop gave order, that in case the priest might choose the better half (they being commonly greedy) that it should go about so, as that the half which the bishop had one year the priest should have the next year, and continued so till brought into the crown rental; since which time they go not about, but still retain that name. All these Umboth rents were also in the year 1664 disponed by Spynie to severalls in few, for the yearly payment of a certain few duty yearly in money for each parish; excepting the parishes of Unst and Fetlor, which no man would few because much of the lands there are still ley, and ley-lands pay no sort of rent, but the few duty must have been paid yearly, so the umboth rents of those parishes are still contained in the crown rental, and are collected by the chamberlain, as the scat is all payable in butter and oil. All these crown rents foresaid are payable in the subsequent year, which often proves detrimental to the rents, because the tenant has the first year free of rent; but when he goes out of the land, he has two years rent to pay for the last year's crops, and the tenant becoming insolvent, as they frequently do, the rent is lost in whole or in part.

5th. Species of crown rent is that called the *watle rent*, which

which is a corrupt contraction of two Danish words; viz.
nuit laugh, i. e. a night laying, the origin whereof is said
to be, that in time of popery the bishop of Orkney and
Zetland sent over a venerable matron, whom he recom-
mended as a person of such extraordinary sanctity, that
upon her lying but one night in every parish in the country,
they would thereafter be blessed with great plenty of corn
and fishing, provided she was rewarded with some small
annual pension during her life, which the simple superstitious inhabitants easily believed; and she having
travelled through the country, and lodged at least a night
in every parish, returned to Orkney, with the grant of a
small sum to be paid her yearly out of every parish in
Zetland during her life, for her prayers in their behalf, and
out of respect to the bishop's desire in her favour. How
long this matron lived I know not; but the contribution
for her was yearly collected for her by the bishop's chamberlain, and for the right proportioning the quota of each
parish they laid so much upon each mark land in the
parish. But when Robert Stewart earl of Orkney came
to be proprietor of the bishop's rents of Orkney and Zetland, finding there had formerly been such a payment, he
put it to his rental, and caused the inhabitants to pay it
yearly, and it has ever since been paid under the denomination of the watle rent, and amounts to about fifty pounds
sterling a year. It is payable at Lammas in the present
year in money; but it would seem that some of the heritors of Zetland, less superstitious and wiser than the rest,
would never pay their quotas thereof, so there are several
roums in each parish where that rent is retained, as never
in use of payment.

6th and last species of payment in the crown rental is
that called the *ox and sheep silver*. This is said to be a
compliment given to the earl of Bothwell, mentioned before, when he was in Zetland, of an ox and 12 sheep out of
every parish in the country for the maintenance of his
family; but seems rather to be a tax imposed upon the
country by Robert and Patric Stewarts earls of Orkney;
for they were the first that made it an annual payment,
and

and put it in their rental, and it is proportioned upon the mark lands in each parish, amounting yearly to about twenty pounds sterling; but there are several relations of it, as of the watle, never in use of payment; it is payable at Lammas in the present year in money. This is the denomination under which the crown rents of Zetland are yearly paid, and what the whole may annually amount to can be no other ways certainly computed than as it stands in the rental thereof, being most of it paid in butter and oil, so these rents are yearly more or less, according to the prices these commodities give, and as the lands are improven; but there is always a considerable discount upon the rental charge.

The land rent payable yearly to the heritors and fewers is only that called *land meals*, formerly paid in butter and wad-mill, now paid in butter and money, in the present year, the butter at Lammas, and the money at Martinmass, each mark land paying so much; but these mark lands are not alike in the rent; but according to what pennies the mark, the land is, as that called twelve *pennie land*, which is the dearest, pays the marks of butter, 16 shillings Scots of Wad-mill, and 8 shillings said money of grassums; 10 pennie land pays each mark 14 mark and ⅔ of a mark of butter, 14 shillings 8 pennies of wad-mill, and 8 shillings of grassums; 9 pennie land pays 12 marks of butter, 12 shillings of wad-mill and 8 shillings of grassums; 8 pennie land pays 10 marks and ⅔ of a mark of butter, 10 shillings 8 pennies of wad-mill, and 8 shillings of grassums; 7 pennie land pays 9 marks ⅓ of of a mark of butter, nine shillings and 4 pennies of wad-mill, and 8 shillings of grassums; 6 pennie land pays 8 marks of butter, and 8 shillings of wad-mill, and 8 shillings of grassums; and 4 pennie land, which is the lowest, pays 6 marks of butter, 6 shillings of wad-mill, and 8 shillings of grassums; and some lands pay no grassums, and others nothing but the butter debt; the crown lands pay after the same manner, but all in the subsequent year as noticed before. The lands in Zetland, for the most part, are not very improveable, and the landlords generally take the wrong way for encouraging their tenants

to

to improve the lands : for it is the common practice with many of them, if they see the tenant thriving, and by his industry becoming richer than his neighbour, he must be warned to remove, unless he will pay more rent yearly, or a large entry for a short tack, and when that tack is out he is again where he was, and must pay a new entry or remove. This makes many tenants careless, nay even averse to improve; whereas, were those tenants that are frugal and industrious encouraged by long tacks and entitled to the benefit of their own improvement, during the improver's life, without any augmentation of the rent, the landlord after the improver's death might set that land to another for a greater rent than it formerly paid, on account of the improvement, and give the next tenant the same encouragement to improve, for it is not to be expected, that any tenant should be so self-denyed as to labour heartily for the interest of the landlord unless he find his own account in it.

There are no doubt abundance of trifling curiosities and old fabulous traditions in Zetland, that some would have thought worth the relating ; but neither my genius, nor intended brevity, will permit me to enter upon that subject.

APPENDIX.

NUMBER I.

Spynie's CHARTER *granted to the Heritors of* ZETLAND *upon their Udell lands.*

TO all and sundrie whom it effeirs, to whose knowledge this present charter shall come, ALEXANDER DOUGLAS, of Spynie, factor, commissioner, principal chamberlain, and trustee of the earldom of Orkney, and lordship of Zetland, greeting in God everlasting; for as mickle as our sovereign lord the king's majesty be his charter of donation under the great seal of Scotland, of the date at Whitehall, the twenty-third day of April, one thousand six hundred and sixty-two years, hath given, granted, disponed, and confirmed, to a noble lord George viscount of Grandison, his heirs, assigns, and successors, under reversion therein mentioned, all and heall the said earldom of Orkney and lordship of Zetland, lying within the said kingdom of Scotland, with all and sundry lordships, baronies, isles, castles, courts, fortalices, manor places, houses, biggings, and others particularly therein specified, together with the lands called Udell lands, lying within the said earldom and lordship of Zetland, with power to the said noble viscount, his heirs and assigns, foresaid, to sell and dispone, in heritable few farm, any part of the said earldom and lordships, udell-lands, and others foresaid belonging thereto, to be holden of the said George viscount of Grandison, his said heirs, successors, and assignies, during the not redemption of the said earldom and lordship; and after the lawful redemption thereof, when it shall happen, of our sovereign lord the king's majesty, and his majesty's heirs and successors, in few farm and heritage, heritable and inredeemable for ever, according to the present rental, and without diminution thereof, as the said charter of donation, containing therein divers and sundry other powers, privileges, immunities, clauses, and conditions, with precept, and instrument of sasine following thereupon, at more length bears: Likeas the said George viscount of Grandison be his commission of the date the said 23rd day of April, and year aforesaid, did nominate and appoint John Earl of Middletown,

town, William duke of Hamilton, Sir Andrew Ramsay of Abbotshall, knight, and William, earl of Morton, lord Dalkeith and Aberdour, to be his trustees for managing the affairs of the said earldom and lordship; and hath given them, or any quorum of them, or their commissioner in their names, all full power and commission thereby for managing the affairs of the same, as the said noble viscount could do therein himself if he were personally present, as the said commission of the date aforesaid at more length purports; and siklike, the said John earl of Middletown, and remnant trustees above designed by their factorie and commission of the date the 7th day of Frebruary, 1663 years last by past, having given full power and commission to me Alexander Douglas of Spynie, to be their factor, commissioner, principal chamberlain, and baillie of the said earldom and lordship, and to set out in few farm the lands, isles, udell-lands, teynds, and others foresaid belonging thereto, and lying within the same, for augmentation of the rental, without diminution thereof as said is, as also to enter and receive fewers, vassals, and tenants of the said lands, and to uplift and receive from them their few duties, composition, and other casualities due therefore; to compound, transact, and agree there anent, and to do every other thing there anent, that the said noble trustees, or their said constituent could do therein themselves, if they were personally present to act therein, as in the said factory and commission of the date above written at more length is contained. And now I understanding, and being perfectly informed that A. B. by himself, his authors and predecessors, and their tenants of the lands after specified, has right and possession of all and sundry Udell-lands, particularly under-written, of whose right and possession of all and sundry udell-lands aforesaid I being no ways willing to prejudge him, but rather to grant unto him, his heirs, and assigns, a more perfect right and security of the same: Therefore, and for augmentation of the rental thereof, as also for a certain sum of money paid and delivered unto me by the said A. B. whereof I grant the receipt, and discharge him thereof, renouncing all exception of the law that can be proponed to the contrary: To have given, granted in heritable and perpetual few ferm, set, and let, and by this my present charter confirmed: Like as I by the tenor hereof give, grant, in heritable few ferm, set and let, and by this my present charter, confirm to the said A. B. his heirs assignies, whatsomever heritable, all and sundry his udell-lands after mentioned possessed by him, and his authors and tenants in their name: All and heall   mark land   pennys the mark in the room of   &c. with the houses, biggings, yeards, tofts, crofts, town malls, quoys, quoy lands, utbracks, nesses, isles, holms, skerries, annexes, connexes, parts, pendicls, and heall pertinents whatsomever, of all and sundry the said lands, all lying within the isles and parishes respective foresaid

lordship

lordship of Zetland, and sheriffdom of Orkney and Zetland, to
be held in, and to be had, all and heall the said lands, with the
pertinents lying, as said is, by the said A. B. his heirs and assignies
whatsomever, of the said noble lord George viscount of Grandison,
his heirs, assigns, and successors, during the not redemption of
the said earldom and lordship, and after their lawful redemption
thereof, when it shall happen, of our sovereign lord the king's
majesty, and his majesty's heirs and successors, in few ferm and
heritage for ever, by all right mithes, and marches, as the same
lies in length and breadth, in houses, biggings, yeards, tofts,
crofts, quoys, quoy lands, hills, dales, nesses, holms, limestone
quarries, mortar, clay, fewel, feal, divots, thack heather, peats,
peat moss, meadows grass, and with power to make utbracks or
setts, foulds, garrths, ways, water stanks, burns, stripes, fowling,
fishing in fresh water, and salt waters, tang waire, out freedom,
in freedom, pastour, leasour, and with common pasture, freesh
and entry, and with all and sundry other freedoms, commodities,
liberties, privileges, profits, easements, and righteous pertinents
whatsomever, as well not named as named, under the earth as
above the same, far or near, from the highest in the hill to the
lowest in the ebb, pertaining to the said lands, and others above
specified, with their pertinents, or that shall righteously be known
to pertain and belong thereto in any manner of way, freely,
quietly, wholly, well, and in peace, but revocation, contradiction,
or again calling whatsomever : Paying therefore yearly the said
A. B. his heirs and successors, or assignies foresaid to the said
noble lord George viscount of Grandison, his heirs, assigns, and
successors, their factors or chamberlains, in their names, and that
during the not redemption of the said earldom and lordship ; and
after the lawful redemption thereof, whenever the same shall
happen, to our said sovereign lord the king's majesty, and his
majesty's heirs and successors, their taxmen, factors, chamberlain's
and others, in their names, conform to use and wont the scat and
wattle duties in use to be paid forth of the said lands, conform to
the rental at terms of payment and parts accustomed in name of
few farm, together with the sum of three shillings four pennies
Scots money, at the first of Martinmass yearly, in augmentation
of the rental thereof, more than ever the same lands paid before ;
together also with the sum of 10 marks money foresaid, at the
entry of every heir to the said lands, in name of doubling the few
farm duty, by and autour the same few farm duty allenerly, and
the said A. B. and his foresaids, giving suit and presence to an
head court to be holden by the said noble viscount and his foresaids, or others, having power from his majesty after the redemption foresaid, and their deputes in their names ; at Scalloway
castle yearly, with this special provision always, like as it is
provided by express condition hereof, in case it shall happen the
said A. B. his heirs and assignies foresaid to fail in making good
and

and thankful payment of the few ferm duties of the foresaid lands and augmentation thereof above written, so that three years run, in the fourth together unpaid, this present charter shall be null and of none avail, for a strength or effect as if the same had never been made. And I for sueth, the said Alexander Douglas of Spynie, my heirs and successors, all and sundry the forenamed lands ; viz. All and heall the said   marks of land, in   &c. with the houses, biggings, yeards, tofts, crofts, town-malls, quoys, quoylands, utbracks, holms, skerries, nesses, annexes, connexes, parts, pendicls, and apertinents, of all and sundry the said lands lying within the foresaid islands, parishes, respective lordship, and sheriffdom above written, to the said A.B. his heirs and assignies whatsomever heritable, from all perils, dangers, and inconveniencies whatsomever, proceeding of my own proper fact and deed allenarly, in and by all things in form and effect, as is above written shall warrant, acquit, and defend, autour to my lovets and ilk any of yours, &c. to the said A.B. or his certain procutor, or attorney, bearer hereof, by deliverance of earth and stone of the ground of the said   mark land, in I decern and ordain to stand and be a sufficient sasine in all time coming, for all the lands and others above-written, with the pertinents, notwithstanding the same lies not contiguous together, but in divers different places, parishes, and isles, where anent I have dispenced, and hereby dispences with for ever, conform to the tenor of this above written charter, and this in no ways you leave undone, &c. In witness whereof, to this present charter, containing precept of sasine, in the end thereof, written by   subscribed with my hand, my seal is appended at   the   day of   1664, before these witnesses A.D.

NUMBER II.

Spynie's Few Charter granted to the fewers of the Crown-land in Zetland.

To all and sundry whom it effeirs, to whose knowledge this present charter shall come. Alexander Douglas of Spynie, factor, commissioner, principal chamberlain, and trustee of the earldom of Orkney and lordship of Zetland, greeting in GOD everlasting, for so much as our sovereign lord the king's majesty, by his charter of donation under the great seal of Scotland, of the date at Whitehall, the 23d day of April 1662, hath given, granted, disponed, and confirmed, to a noble lord George viscount of Grandison, his heirs, assignies, and successors, under reversion therein mentioned, all and heall the said earldom of Orkney and lordship of Zetland, lying within the said kingdom of Scotland, with all

and

and sundry lordships, baronies, isles, castles, courts, fortalices, manor places, houses, biggings, and others particularly therein specified, together with the lands called Udell-lands, lying within the said earldom and lordship, with power to the said noble viscount, his heirs and assignies foresaid, to sell and dispone in heritable and perpetual few farm any part of the said earldom and lordships, udell-lands, and others foresaid belonging thereto, to be holden of the said George viscount of Grandison, his said heirs, successors, and assignies, during the not redemption of the said earldom and lordship, and after the lawful redemption thereof, when it shall happen, of our sovereign lord the king's majesty, and his majesty's heirs and successors, in few farm and heritage, heritable and irredeemable for ever, according to the present rental, and without diminution thereof, as the said charter of donation, containing thereuntil divers and sundry other powers, privileges, immunities, clauses, and conditions, with precept and instrument of sasine following thereupon, at more length bears.   Like as the said George viscount of Grandison, by his commission of the date the said 23d day of April and year foresaid, did nominate and appoint John earl of Middletown, William duke of Hamilton, Sir Andrew Ramsay of Abbots-hill, knight, and William earl of Morton, lord Dalkeith and Aberdour, to be his trustees for managing the affairs of the said earldom and lordship, and hath given them, or any quorum of them, or their commissioner in their name, as full power and commission thereby for managing the affairs of the same, as the said noble viscount could do therein himself if he were personally present, as the said commission of the date foresaid at more length proports : And sik like the said John earl of Middletown, William duke of Hamilton, and remnant trustees above designed by their factory and commission of the date of the 20th of February, 1665, last by past, having given full power and commission to me the said Alexander Douglas, of Spynie, to be their factor commissioner, principal chamberlain, and baillie of the said earldom and lordship, and to set out in few farm the land, isles, udell-lands, tiends, and others belonging thereto, and lying within the same, for augmentation of the rental, without diminution thereof as said, as also to enter and receive fewers, vassalls, and tenants of the said lands, and to uplift and receive from them, their few duties, compositions, and other casualties due therefrom, to compound, transact, and agree there anent, and to do every other thing there anent, that the said noble trustees, or their constituent, could do therein themselves, if they were personally present to act therein, as in the said factory and commission of the date above written at more length is contained.   And now I understanding perfectly, that the end and cause of setting out of lands, and others above written, in few farm, is for the better improvement thereof, and that conform to the laudable laws of the realm made anent planting and policy,

the

the same may be the better decerned and brought through the
pains and industry of frugal and virtuous people to the more
fertility, and knowing likewise that the lands and others after
specified were never set in few farm of before, therefore and for
augmentation of the rental thereof, as also for a certain sum of
money paid and delivered to me by A. B. wherewith I hold me
well content, satisfied and paid, and discharge him of the same,
renouncing all exceptions of the law that can be proponed, or
alledged in the contrary, to have given, granted in heritable and
perpetual few farm set and letten ; and by this my present charter
confirm, like as I by the tenor hereof, give, grant, in heritable and
perpetual few farm, set and let, and be this my present charter,
confirm to the said A. B. his heirs and assignies whatsomever
heritable, all and heall   markland   pennys the
mark in the room of   &c. with the houses, biggings, yeards,
holms, nesses, tofts, crofts, town molls, quoys, quoylands, utbracks,
annexes, connexes, and pertinants whatsomever pertaining thereto,
lying within the parish of   lordship of Zetland, and sherriff-
dom of Orkney and Zetland, to be holden and to be had all and
heall the said   markland in   &c. with the
houses, biggings, and pertinants thereto belonging, lying as is
above-mentioned, to the said A. B. and his heirs and assignies
whatsomever, of the said George viscount of Grandison, his heirs
and successors, during the not redemption of the said earldom and
lordship, and after the lawful redemption thereof, when it shall
happen, of our sovereign lord the king's majesty, his highnesses
heirs and successors, in few farm fee and heritage for ever, be all
right marches, and divided as the same lies in length and breadth,
the houses, biggings, yeards, holms, nesses, tofts, crofts, town
molls, quoys, quoy lands, meadows, mosses, muirs, ways, waters,
stanks, lochs, burns, stripes, hills, dales, fowling, fishing in fresh
water and salt, peats, peat moss, cunings, cuningyers, doves, dove-
cots, links, limestone quarry, grass, wair, out freedom, in freedom,
pastour, leisure, with common pasture free ish and entrie, and
with all and sundry commodities, privileges, easements, profits,
and righteous pertinents, as well not named as named, under the
earth as above, far as near pertaining, or that justly shall be known
to pertain and belong to the same lands, and others above specified,
in any manner of way, freely, quietly, well, and in peace ; but
any impediment, obstacle, contradiction, or again calling whatsomever, paying therefore yearly the said A. B. his said heirs and
assignies, to the said George viscount of Grandison, his heirs,
assignies, and successors, factors, chamberlains, servitors, and
others in their name, during the not redemption of the said
earldom and lordship, and after the lawful redemption thereof,
when it shall happen, to our said sovereign lord the king's majesty,
his highnesses's heirs and successors, their factors, chamberlains,
and others, in their name, the land mealls and duties justly
                                        adibeted,

adibeted, and yearly payable forth therewith, conform to the rental ; viz. the number and quantity of   lispounds of butter, or 48 shillings Scots for each lispound of butter, with the sum of   pounds Scots money, as for the land mailes of the heall above named lands, with the pertinents, together also with the scat and wattle, and other accustomed duties likeways due payable forth of the same, conform to the rental at the terms of payment and ports used and wont, all in name of few farm, and other duties liable and due to be performed by the said A. B. and his foresaids, as use is together, also with the sum of four shillings Scots money, at the term of Martinmas, in augmentation of the rental thereof, more than ever the same paid before, and also giving of suit and presence to the three head courts, to be held in the said noble viscount and his foresaids, or their deputes, or others, having power from his majesty, after the redemption foresaid, at the town of Scallaway banks yearly, and to all other courts to be holden by them, when they shall be lawfully warned thereto, and the heirs of the said A. B. paying to the said noble viscount and his foresaids, during the not redemption as above specified, the sum of   money foresaid, the first year of their entry to the said lands, and other above specified in the name of doubling the said few farm duties, and that by and attilour the same few farm duties, and other above written, for all other burdens, actions, demands, or service secullor, that of the same lands, and others, with the pertinents thereof above expressed in any ways, may be asked or required : Providing always, like as it is hereby especially provided, that in case it shall happen the said A. B. and his foresaids, do fail in making good and thankful payment of the said few farm duty yearly, with the scat and wattle, and augmentation above-mentioned, so that it happen two years to run, and the third unpaid then, and in that case this present few farm charter shall be null and of none avail, force, strength, nor effect, as if the same had never been made nor granted.   And I forthwith, the said Alexander Douglas, of Spynie, my heirs and successors, all and heall the said   mark land, in   &c. with the heall houses, biggings, yeards, holms, nesses, parts, pendicles, and pertinents thereof whatsomever, lying in the said parishes within the said lordship of Zetland, to the said A. B. his heirs and assignies foresaid, from all perils, dangers, and inconveniences whatsomever, proceeding of my own proper fact and deed alternately, in all and by all things, in form and effect, as is above specified shall warrant, acquit and defend : Autour, To my lovits   and every one of you, my baillies, in that part conjunctly and severally constitute, greeting, it is my will and I charge you, that incontinant after sight hereof ye pass, exhibit, give, and deliver heritable state and sasine, actual, real, and corporal possession of all and heall the said   marks of land in   &c. with the houses, biggings,

biggings, &c. and this in no ways, &c. In witness whereof to this my present charter, containing precept of sasine in the end thereof. Written by, &c. and subscribed with my hand, my seal being apendit at   the   day of   1664, before these witnesses. A.D.

NUMBER III.

The Queen's Gift of the Islands of ORKNEY *and* ZETLAND *to the Right Honourable the Earl of* MORTON.

OUR Sovereign Lady, considering, that forasmuch as her majesty and the estates of parliament, by their act and disposition, of the date the 12th day of February instant, and for the good and weighty causes therein mentioned, for all right or title any way competent to the crown or principality of Scotland, have dissolved and thereby dissolve, from the crown and patrimony thereof, all and haill the earldom of Orkney and lordship of Zetland, with all and sundry isles, holms, burghs, udell-lands, and other lands whatsomever, of what name and by what designation the same are or may be known, lying within the sheriffdom or steuartrie of Orkney, and pertaining to the said earldom and lordship, and by the acts of annexation passed in the parliaments held in the years 1612 and 1669, pertaining to her Majesty, or by whatever other right or title, together with all castles, towers, fortalices, milns, multers, fishings, arents, reversions, patronages of kirks, chaplanries, alterages or prebendries, teinds, parsonage or vicarage, with the office of justiciary, sheriffship, stewartship, bailliary, and foudery, with the casualities and privileges thereto belonging, together with all other parts, pendicles, and pertinents, casualities, jurisdictions, privileges, and others whatsomever belonging to the same, to the effect her Majesty might dispone to her Majesty's right, trustee, and well-beloved cousin and counsellor James earl of Morton, his heirs and successors whatsomever, the said earldom, lordship, isles, lands, milns, offices, jurisdictions, casualities, and other above-mentioned, or any other part thereof, and that in such manner as may most effectually preserve the same to the said earl and his foresaids, for support of the family of Morton, redeemable by her Majesty, and her royal successors, on payment of 30,000 pounds sterling, extending to 36,000 pounds Scots money ; and that in due and competent form, to be holden all and sundry the foresaid earldom, lordship, isles, lands, milns, burghs, tiends, patronage, offices, jurisdictions, casualities, and others above written, with the pertinents, to the said James earl of Morton, and his foresaids, of her Majesty and her royal successors, giving yearly the said James earl of Morton and his foresaids, to her said Majesty and her royal successors, during the not redemption for

all

all and sundry the foresaid earldom, isles, holms, udell-lands, and other lands, milns, burghs, teinds, patronages, offices, jurisdictions, and others above-mentioned, with the pertinences the sum of 6000 pounds Scots money, at two terms in the year, Whitsunday and Martinmass, be equal portions in name of few farm, with the double of the said few duty at the entry of every heir, and administration of justice to all and sundry her Majesty's leidges, in the aforesaid offices, as accords with the sum of 1600 pounds Scots money, to the ministers of Orkney, or such other sums as are or shall be modified by way of augmentation to the said ministers out of the tiends above disponed, at the terms of payment used and wont for all other burden, exaction, question, demand, or secular service, which may be any way asked or required forth of the said earldom, lordship, isles, lands, offices, jurisdictions, and others above mentioned, during the not redemption, reserving all hawks pertaining to her majesty, with the faulconaries, salaries, and other casualities to them belonging, conform to former customs used and wont; and lastly, her Majesty, with advice and consent foresaid, declared and ordained the right to be granted by her majesty and her royal successors to the said earl and his foresaids, of the premises dissolved to the effect and in manner foresaid, to be also valid and effectual, as if the same had never been annexed to the crown and patrimony thereof, and as the said earldom, lordship, isles, lands, and others, foresaid were there particularly enumerate about the same, be not so done, whereanent her Majesty with advice and consent foresaid, by the said act of Dissolution, has dispenced for ever, and her Majesty with advice and consent foresaid statutes and declares, that the said act of Dissolution should have the full force and strength of any former act of Dissolution past in the best form with all clauses needful; and rescinded and repelled the foresaid acts of parliament past in the said years 1612 and 1669, and all other acts annexing the foresaid earldom of Orkney and lordships of Zetland, isles, lands, offices, jurisdictions, and others, particularly and generally abovementioned, to the crown, and the heall heads, articles, and clauses, thereof, in so far as the same might be hurtful and prejudicial to the foresaid act of Dissolution, and rights to follow thereon, declaring always, that the right and jurisdiction of admiralty is not therein comprehended as the said act of Disolution more fully proports. Therefore and in prosecution of the said act of parliament, and especially that her majesty may give a mark of her royal justice and favour to the said James earl of Morton and his family, for preserving the same, our said sovereign lady, with advice and consent of her majesty's right trusty and entirely beloved cousins and counsellors James duke of Queensberry, her Majesty's high commissioner of her ancient kingdom of Scotland, James earl of Seafield lord high chancellor of the said kingdom, James marquis of Montrose president of her Majesty's privy council, James earl of Galloway,

Archibald

Archibald earl of Forfar, David earl of Glasgow lord treasurer depute, William lord Ross, and Mr. Francis Montgomery of Giffan, lords commissioners of her Majesty's treasury, comptrollers and treasury of new augmentation; and also with the special advice and consent of the lords and others commissioners of her majesty's exchequer of the forcsaid kingdom, ordains a charter to be past and exped, under her majesty's great seal of the kingdom of Scotland, in due form, giving, granting, selling, annalizing, and in few ferm disponing like as her majesty, by these presents, gives, grants, sets, annalizes, and dispones, in few farm, and for her majesty, and her royal successors, with consent foresaid, perpetually confirms to the said James earl of Morton, and his heirs male whatsomever succeeding to him in his honour and dignity, whilks failing to his heirs and assignies whatsomever heritable, with and under the reversion and redemption after specified, all and heall the said earldom of Orkney and lordship of Zetland, lying within the said kingdom of Scotland, with all and sundry the lands, lordships, regalities, barronies, isles, castles, towers, fortalicies, manner places, houses, biggings, yeards, orchards, parks, ferms, milns, miln lands, multers, knaveships, woods, fishings as well of salmon as of other fishes in fresh and salt water, freedoms, grassums for entries, towns, burghs, arents, ferm duties, few farms, together with all and sundry lands, called Udell-lands, lying within the said earldoms, lordship, and isles of the same, with all and sundry privileges, casualities, and commodities whatsomever pertaining thereunto, either by sea or land, with tenants, tenantries, service of free tenents, as well to teinds bourgh as land teinds, great and small, parsonage, and vicarage teind duties, advocations, donations, and right of patronage of kirk and chaplanarie, alterages and prebendries, within the said earldom and lordship, isles, udell-lands, and others thereto belonging; together likewise with the heritable office of justiciary sherriffship, or stewartship, bailliearie and fouderie within the said earldom and lordship, isles, and others foresaid, belonging to the samen, with wrack and ware, together with all and sundry privileges, liberties, fees, casualities, and other commodities whatsoever belonging to the said office of justiciary, sherriffship or stuartship, bailliearie and fouderie, or any of them, with full power to the said James earl of Morton and his foresaids, to set, affix, affirm, hold and continue justiciar, sheriff, or steuart baillie and foudery courts at whatsomever place or places within the heall bounds of the said earldom, lordship isles, lands, and others, foresaid, most convenient for that effect, and to make, create, and constitute, justice, sheriff, stewart, baillie, and foudery deputes, with clarks, procurator, fiscalls, officers, serjants, dempsters, and other members of court, needful for holding the said justiciar, sherriff, stewart, baillie, and foudery courts, within the heall bounds of the said earldom, lordship, isles and lands, and other above written, pertaining thereto,

thereto, and to do every other thing necessary and requisite there anent, as fully and freely in all respects as any other justiciar, sheriff, stuart, baillie, or foudery within the said kingdom of Scotland, isles of Orkney and Zetland, has done or may do by virtue of their office, at any time byegone or to come. Like as her majesty, with consent aforesaid, by these presents, gives, grants, and dispones to the said James earl of Morton, and his foresaids in all time comming her right of the few and other duties, casualties, and services of all and sundry the heritable vassals and others within the said earldom, lordship, isles, lands, and others foresaid, with full and sole power to the said James earl of Morton, and his foresaids, in her majesty's place, as remaining still their immediate superior to enter and receive the said heritable vassals, who now actually hold of her Majesty, and the crown, and their heirs to grant charter and infeftments to whatsomever person or persons of the said earldom, lordship, isles, lands, and others above written, with the pertinents, or any part thereof, upon resignation or disposition of the said vassal, or decreet of sale, appressing or ajudication from them; and that either by confirmation or charter, containing precept of sasine, and to uplift, intromit with, uplift and dispose upon all and sundry the casualties of the said vassals already vacant, and not disponed, or which shall happen to fall or vauk hereafter, in all time coming, by single or liferent escheat, non-entry, recognition, or any other manner of way, without prejudice, always to the said earl and his foresaids, of the superiorities, and all casualties, of all and such vassals and others, who formerly held of the earl of Orkney, and do now hold of her majesty; it is also with full power and free liberty to the said vassals who now hold of her majesty to return and take their holdings of the said earl of Morton and his foresaids, as before they held the same of the earls of Orkney, in their option, together with all right, title, interest, claim of right, property, and possession, petitor and possessor, with her majesty, her predecessors or successors had, as or any ways may have, ask, claim, or pretend, to the said earldom, lordship, udell lands, teinds, patronages, milns, offices, and others, above disponed, with the pertinents, or to the few duties, maills, fairms, carns, customs, casualties, services, profits, and other duties of the same, for the terms of Whitsunday and Martinmas 1707 years, and that for the crop and year of God 1707 foresaid, and of all years and terms thereafter to come, during the not-redemption under-written, by reason of ward non-entry, relief eschet, escheat life rent, forfaultry disclamation, bastardie last aire, last aire allination, of the whole, or most part, reduction of infeftments, sasines, and retours, not showing of holdings, not payment of by gone duties, want of confirmation, or by virtue of whatsoever acts of annexation, acts of parliaments, laws, statutes, or constitutions, made or to be made, or any other manner of way, right, or title whatsomever, cause, deed, fact, or occasion,

casion, preceding the date of thir presents, renouncing, transfering, and over-giving the heall right of the premises, during the not-redemption under-written, to and in favour of the said James earl of Morton, and his foresaids, with all power to him and them, to pursue and suit the right and benefit of the heall premises, and to ask, crave, receive, intromit with, and uplift the heall few duties, mealls, farms, kains, customs, casualties, services, profits, and other duties above disponed, and to grant gifts, tacks, assignations, translations, and other rights and conveyances thereof, or of any part of the same, and to call and pursue therefore as accords, compon, transact and agree there anent, and to grant acquittances, renunciations, and discharges thereof, which shall be sufficient to the receivers, and generally all and sundry things in and concerning the premises to do, use, and exerse such like, and as fully in all respects as her Majesty, or any of her royal predecessors or successors have done, might have done, or may do themselves : And further, her Majesty has united, created, erected, and incorporated, and by these presents, for herself and her highnesses successors, with consent aforesaid, unites, creates, erects, and incorporates, all and sundry the foresaid lands, lordship, towns, udell lands, isles, teinds, and others, foresaid castles, towers, fortalices, maner, places, woods, grassums, fishings, milns, milnlands, yeards, orchards, parks, fermes, fore entries, towns, burghs, offices, patronages, and others above specified, with the pertinents, in an heall and free earldom and lordship, and baronie, with the privilege of justiciary, sheriffship, or stuartrie, bailiarie, or foudery respective to be called now, and in all time coming, the earldom of Orkney and lordship of Zetland, and her Majesty wills and grants, and for her Majesty and her royal successors, with consent foresaid, descerns and ordains, that an sasine, now to be taken by the said James earl of Morton, and his heirs male above mentioned, which failing as said is, in all time coming, at the castle of Kirkwall, or upon any part of the ground of the said lands, earldom and lordship, shall stand, and be a valid and sufficient sasine to him and them for the said heall earldom, lordship, lands, baronies, isles, udell lands, milns, teinds, tacks, patronages, offices, and others respective, particularly and generally above written, with the heall pertinents thereof, notwithstanding that the same be of divers names and designations, and that the same lies not contiguous together, but in separate isles, where anent, her Majesty has dispenced, and be these presents, with consent foresaid, dispences for ever : Providing always, like as it is hereby provided and declared, and shall be provided and declared, by the charter and infeftment to follow hereon, that it shall be leisom, leisom and lawful to her Majesty, and her royal successors, at any terms of Whitsunday or Martinmas, hereafter following ; upon the premonition of 60 days preceding to be made to the said James earl of Morton, and his foresaids, personally at their dwelling places, in presence of a notar,

and

and witnesses, to redeem the foresaid earldom of Orkney and lordship of Zetland, by real payment making to the said James earl of Morton, and his foresaids, of the said full sum of 30,000 pounds sterling money; upon payment of which, the said James earl of Morton, and his foresaids, shall be holden and obliged to renounce in favour of her Majesty, and her royal successors, all right and title they have, or can pretend to, the said earldom and lordship, in all time thereafter, any manner of way whatsomever, with this express condition and provision always, that until the sum, be so redeemed and duly declared, the said earl of Morton, and his foresaids, shall bruck, enjoy, and possess, the said earldom and lordship, and others thereunto pertaining and belonging above written, with the haill maills, few duties, and other duties, profits, and services, and casualities thereof in the same way and manner as if the same had been disponed heritable and irredeemably, and shall be no ways accomptable for his intermissions therewith, nor shall the same be imputed in payment of the foresaid principal sum, as also that the rents and few duties of the year wherein the said redemption shall be declared, and all casualities which do then fall and heall benefit and profit thereof, shall pertain and belong to the said James earl of Morton, to be holden, and to be held all and sundry the foresaid earldom of Orkney and lordship of Zetland, lands, baronies, isles, udell lands, milns, teinds, kirks, patronages, offices, and others above disponed, with the pertinents united and erected as said is to the said James earl of Morton, and his foresaids, during the not-redemption, of our said sovereign lady, and her royal successors, in free earldom, lordship and baronie, with justiciary, sherriffship, stuartrie and bailliarie, and foudery, and heall liberties and privileges thereof, in few farm, fee and heritage for ever, be all right, meiths, and marches thereof, old and divided, as the same lye in the length and breadth, in houses, biggings, mosses, muirs, foreland, pasturages, miln, multers, knaveships, hunting, hawking, fishing, coal, coal-houghs, cunnings, cuningars, doves, dovecats, court plant, herezita, blood wits, with fork-fass, thole thurne, wrack, ware, infang thef, utfang thef, pit and gallows, with all and sundry other privileges, liberties, commodities, easements, common pasturage, free ish and entrie, and others, as well not named as named, under the earth as above, well and in peace, but any reversion or again calling whatsomever: Giving therefore yearly the said James earl of Morton and his foresaids, and his heirs male whatsomever, succeeding to him in his honour and dignity, which failing his heirs and assignies whatsomever, during the not redemption above written, to our soverign lady and royal successors, for all and sundry the foresaid earldom, lordship, baronies, isles, udell lands, and other lands, milns, tiends, tacks, patronages, offices, and others, above disponed, with the pertinents, unite, and incorporate, as said is, the sum of 6000 pounds Scots, at two terms in the

year

year, Whitsunday and Martinmas, be equal portions, in name of few farm duty, with the double of the said few farm at the entry of every heir to the said earldom, lordship, isles, and others foresaid, and administration of Justice, to all and sundry her Majesty's liedges in the foresaid offices as accords, with the sum of 1600 pounds to the ministers of Orkney or such other sum or sums as are or shall be modified by way of augmentation to the said ministers, out of the teinds above disponed, at the terms of payment used and wont, together with the hawks belonging to her Majesty and the falconers sallaries conform to formed custom used and wont; for all other burden, exaction, question, demand, or secular services, which may any way be asked or required furth of the said earldom, lordship, isles, lands, offices, jurisdictions, tiends, and others above-mentioned; and lastly, her Majesty faithfully promises on the word of a princess, to cause ratify these presents charter and sasine to follow thereupon in the present or the next session of this her majesty's current parliament, or any other ensuing parliament, for doeing whereof, the foresaid charter shall be a sufficient warrant; and that the said charter be further extended in the best and most ample form, containing precepts of sasine, and all other clauses; and that precepts be orderly direct hereupon in form, as effeirs, given at her Majesty's court of Kensington, the 1st day of February, 1706-7, and of her Majesty's reign the fifth year, ' Ut supra scribitur ANNE R.; et subscribitur Queensberrie, commissioner; Seafield, canseller; Montrose et Gallaway, Forfar; Glasgow et Montgomerie, Mar.; S. Louden, S. Weems, Northesk, Leven, Cromerty, James Murray, Archi. Douglas, John Erskine, comps, ten marks.

NUMBER IV.

The old Country Acts, or Abridgements thereof.

Act 1. THAT the baillie in each parish concur and assist in the discipline of the kirk and execution thereof.

2. That none miscarry or lay down the cross under a penalty of ten pounds Scots, *totious quotious.*

3. That all weights and measures be yearly adjusted, marked, and observed, conform to the several acts made there anent, under the pains of ten pounds, and doubling thereof as often as contravined.

4. That all thiggers of wool, corn, fish, and others, be apprehended wherever they come, by any that can find them, and to put them in firmance, to be punished with the stocks and joggs; and that none receive them in their houses, nor give them hospitality or service, under the pain of ten pounds, *to. qu.*

5. Annent destroying of ravens, corbies, &c. in manner and under the pains in the act of parliament made there anent.

6.

6. That good neighbourhood be observed and keeped by timous and sufficient bigging of decks, and putting up of grinds and passages, keeping and closing the same ; and that none big up accustomed grinds or passages through towns, or any close up the king's high road, under the pain of ten pounds ; that all decks be sufficiently built before the last of March so as all cattle may be kept without decks from the time that the labouring begins ; and whatsoever person shall wilfully allow their cattle to tread upon their neighbour's ploughed land or meadows, before the first of May, shall pay for each swine ten shillings, for each sheep two shillings, for each horse, mare, or colt six shillings ; doubling the said pains after the first of May, besides payment of the damages ; and that they pay forty shillings for each winter slop found in their decks after the first of May : That whoever neglects to close the grinds, or breaks down, or goes over decks, shall pay for each time they do so forty shillings Scots, besides the damages ; that all within one deck keep good neighbourhood to others, by thetering, herding, and folding, as well by day as by night, and not to pasture upon, or overlay others with their cattle, nor unlawfully hurd and drive upon others, under the pain of forty shillings for each fault, *to. qu.* beside damages ; and that none have more swine than effeiring to their land labouring ; and that none have swine pasturing upon ther neighbour's land, meadows, grass, commonalty and pasturage, neither within or without decks, that hath no swine pasturing upon them, and that they keep their swine upon their own ground under the pain of ten pounds, by and attour the damages, and that building, punding, and hurding, be used in lawful way before or a little after sun-setting, and that none scare, hurd, or brack up their neighbours punds and buills, under the pain of ten pounds beside damages.

7. That none go into other mens holms or isles under the pain of ten pounds for the first fault, twenty pounds for the second, and for the third to be repute as thieves, and prosecute accordingly ; moreover, by act the 3d of July, 1628, that the said penalties be exacted, and the one-half thereof to be delivered to the judge, and the other half to the dilaters or owners of the holms.

8. That none keep sheep dogs but such as are appointed or allowed by the sheriff or baillie, with the advice of the special honest men in the parish, whose names are to be recorded in the court books, and each of them to be answerable for their actings ; and that none run after sheep with a dog unaccompanied, or take in and kill any until first showing the mark to a rancellman, or other honest man, under the pain of ten pounds Scots money for the first fault, besides payment of damages, and doubling the said pain for the second, and for the third fault to be a point of dity, and the contraviners to be holden and repute as thieves, and discharged to use or keep a sheep-dog, in all times coming ; and that none mark lambs or row sheep where there is different owners

in

in the flock, but at the sight of sufficient witnesses under the pains foresaid; moreover, if any person shall use a sheep-dog, and run therewith after his own sheep amongst those of his neighbours unaccompanied; mark, row, or take home any without showing the same as aforesaid, shall pay for the first fault four angels; for the second six angels; and for the third, or at any time under the cloud of night, shall be holden and repute a common thief, and punished accordingly.

9. That none blood, hurt, or mutilate their neighbour's nolt, sheep, or horses, under the pain of ten pounds Scots, beside payment of damages.

10. That all dogs in the respective parishes, be tried yearly by the bailie or the rancellmen, and other honest men in the parishes; and if they be found to have dogs that take, or may take sheep, who are not allowed to keep sheep-dogs, shall pay according to the former act, and the dogs so found to be hanged, and all running dogs to be discharged, under the pain of forty shillings, to be paid by the owner of the dog, *to. qu.* and the dog to be hanged.

11. That the rancellmen be yearly sworn and examined, or as often as needful, and give an account to the sheriff or baillie anent their diligence; and that they see all wool-skins, heads, and marks whatsomever; and that they see all cloths and stockings made of wool, and compare the same with the stock of the makers; and all lines and tomes made of horse-hair, and keep accounts thereof; and that they take up inventories from Smiths and Websters of all work wrought by them; and that none refuse rancelling, or to give up inventories, or quarrel, or offend at rancelling, under the pain to be repute and punished as thieves.

12. That none see or seduce another man's servant, except they be discharged of their masters, or that they have discharged them forty days before a lawful term, and that none receive such servant who are not free of their service, nor give them hospitality nor entertain them, nor flit them either by land or sea; nor are they to be received, nor entertained, though free, into any other parish, without a testimonial; and that none keep in their houses idle women, vagabonds, or housefolk, nor let houses to such, under the pain of ten pounds, *to. qu.*

13. Act, August 1630, ratifying the former Act, forbidding any person to marry and set up house who has not forty pounds Scots of free gear, or some lawful trade to live by; and that none set house or land to such persons under the pain of ten pounds said money; and that none seduce, force, or transport any other man's son, daughter or servant, forth of the country, under the pain of one hundred pounds Scots money.

14. That none ride, labour, or use, any other man's horse without liberty of the owner, under the pains following, viz. without in the parish where the owner dwells, to pay four marks to the sheriff or baillie, and other four marks to the delators or informers;

and

and from one parish to another to double, trible, and quadruple, the foresaid pain effeirent to the parishes he passes through ; and that none cut away other man's horse-tail or main, under the pain of ten pounds ; moreover 3rd of September, this act ratified, and the contraveners thereof the 2d or 3d time to be punished as thieves.

15. That none hide nor conceal any kind of theft, sorcery, witchcraft, riots, blood, or other injury, and prejudices done, but shall delate and report the same to their baillie, as they will eschew to be repute as partakers thereof, and punished according to law.

16. That the bailie in each parish take order with the trying and adjusting of bismers, with the stoups, cans, and other mets and measures, under the pains contained in the act of parliament ; and that a lispound upon the bismer used for receiving of rent butter, and other merchandise bought and sold, be 28 pound, or one quarter of an hundred weight, allowed by law in all grocery ware ; and that the can wherein the rent oil is measured, as also that used in buying and selling, contain one Scots quart and a mutchkin of water and no more. That the ell on which all coarse cloth, linen, and stuffs are measured, be 3 feet 1 inch, or 37 inches long ; and that the ell called the Websters ell be 3 feet 4 inches, or 40 inches long, on which only unscored cloth is measured.

17. That none row sheep on Sunday, under the pain of ten pounds.

18. That none meddle with other mens goods or gear at their own hand, under pretence of alledged debt, especially the goods in their own keeping, under the pain of ten pounds Scots, besides restoring of the goods with their profits.

19. That none buy victual in wholesale, and retail it at a greater price before publication of eight days warning, under a pain of forty pounds Scots, *to. qu.*

20. That no brewer sell ale dearer, nor effeirent to the price of the malt ; and that it be sufficient drink and measure, under the pain of confiscation.

21. That none mix ale, beer, or wine, under the pain of confiscation.

22. That bounds have no more persons in their families than effeirent to their estates and land labouring, and that they put one or more of them to another master, that needs servants, conform to the ancient form of the country.

23. That none delve, till, take on pasture from their neighbours land or grass, under the pain of 10 pounds Scots, beside the payment of damages.

24. That none repair to feasts uncalled, under the pain of 40 shillings Scots.

25. That poinded goods be loosed within six hours after advertisement, and the sute satisfied, under the pain of 40 shillings
Scots ;

Scots; and being advertised, denies the goods, shall pay 6 pounds
Scots; or if they take them away at their own hand, shall pay 10
pounds Scots.

26. That none remove from land or houses of their own accord,
or shall demolish or take away any thing belonging thereto, although furnished by themselves, under the payment of 20 pounds
beside payment of the damage.

27. That all persons have sufficient corn yard dykes; and that
no mends be made for corn eaten within corn yards, except
where more than one is concerned in the yard; he that hath the
insufficient deck must pay the other's damage; as also for all
marks the owner whereof must pay the damage.

28. That none libb any beast upon Sunday, under the pain of
20 pounds Scots.

29. That all bloods and riots be assithed according to justice.

30. That all briggs and common passages be kept in repair by
the persons used to repair them, under the pain of 10 pounds.

31 That none use staff bismers, nor any other, save such as are
adjusted, and marked to buy and sell on, under the pain of 20
pounds Scots.

32. That every scatald have a sufficient pund, under the pain
of 10 pounds Scots.

33. That none use musel bait, or other bait, but such as all or
most part of the fishers have, under the pain of 10 pounds; and
that none fish with haddock lines within voes, from Belton to
Marts. or so long as they can draw haddocks on hand lines, under
the like pain of 10 pounds Scots; and that none take bait, nor
cut tang in another man's ebb, under the like pain of 10 pounds.

34. That all persons living in neighbourhood, keep order, law,
and good neighbourhood, in tilling, labouring and manuring the
ground, conform to the ancient custom formerly observed, under
the pain of 12 pounds Scots, and failing therein, to be put from
land labouring, and ordered to service.

35. That all horses belonging either to utscatlders or inscatlders,
oppressing and overlaying the neighbourhood, be instantly removed, after due advertisement given to their owners, and at the
kirk door, under the pain of being confiscat and escheat to the king.

36 That none contemptuously pasture upon, rive flawes, cut
floss, or cast peats, in their neighbours scatald, under the pain of
10 pounds Scots, nor that any cut floss before Lammas-day in
their own scatald, without due advertising the neighbours of the
scatald, under the pain of 40 shillings Scots, to. qu. and that
none have more swine than four upon a last of land over winter,
under the pain of ten pounds.

37. That none keep scar sheep, except it be in the holms or
nesses, dickt in, properly belonging to themselves, under the pain
of 10 pounds Scots, and forfeiture of the sheep after six months'
advertisement.

38.

38. That none bring nor teather their horses within the decks of Kirktowns, under the pain of forty shillings Scots, for each time they do so, without liberty asked and granted.

39. That the sheriff of each parish, with twelve honest men there, ride the marches of the parish, betwixt the 1st of October and the last of April, yearly, or when required thereto by the Scatalders, under the pain of forty pounds.

40. That each sheriff have the heall country acts authentikly extracted under the steuart clerks hands, and cause read at least the abreviate thereof in their sheriff courts twice a year, or once at least, that none may pretend ignorance of the same, and take true tryal of the breaches thereof, and cause poynd for the same, and that they find caution for what part thereof may be due to the sheriff, or pror fiscal in his name, and deliver the same to the sheriff at the head court, under the pain of deprivation ; and that each sheriff have an authentic court book, wherein all their acts and process of court shall be written and set down, and that the same be produced to each clerk at the circuit courts kept in the parish, under the pain of deprivation.

41. That none go to sea, or be employed about fishing, from sun set on Saturday nights till sun rising on Monday morning, nor travel by sea or land about their secular affairs or business, or any other way imployed therein on the Sabbath-day, except in works of necessity and mercy, under the pain of 10 pounds Scots, by and attour the penalties and punishments ordained by law against all Sabbath-breakers.

NUMBER V.

The Ferry Fraughts in ZETLAND, *on the East Side.*

	A 6 oar boat. Scots.		A 4 oar boat. Scots.	
From Unst to Fetlor		10		6
Unst to Yeall over Blooma Sound ...		4		2
Uya Sound to Refirth	1	4		15
Uya Sound to Burravoe Yell	2	8	1	10
Fetlor to Refirth		12		8
Fetlor to Burravoe Yell	1	16	1	4
Burravoe Yell to Burnes, or Tofit ...		18		12
Burravoe to Ollaberrie, to No. Roo, the same	1	10	1	
Burravoe to Mavisgrind	2		1	10
Ulsta to Tofit		10		6
West Sandwick to Ollaberie, No. Roo or Queforth		18		12
West Sandwick to Mavisgrind, ...	1	16	1	4
No. Roo to Mavisgrind	1	16	1	4
Olaberie to Mavisgrind	1	4		16
Burravoe to Boatsroum		18		12

From

	A 6 oar boat. Scots.	A 4 oar boat. Scots.
From Burravoe to Luna	1 6	18
Burravoe to Simbester	1 16	1 4
Sullom to Scatsta, 2s. from Ollaberry to Buranes	15	10
Burness, Swnister, or Deall to Luna ...	15	10
Collafrith to Luna	12	8
Luna to Vidlan	6	4
Luna to Whalsay. Whalsay Sound 4 shillings,	12	8
Whalsay to Laxvoe, Bulister, or Neep	12	8
Whalsay to Brough	18	12
Whalsay to Lerwick	1 16	1 4
Vassay to Lerwick	18	14
Catfirth to Lerwick	1	14
Vassay or Catfirth to Laxfirth ...	9	6
The common fare over Brassay Sound, is		2
Laxfirth to Lerwick	1	14
Brewick, or Cold Clift, to Lerwick ...	15	10
Lerwick to Quarf	15	10
Lerwick to Ockraquoy	1 0	15
Lerwick to Aith	1 4	18
Lerwick to Sands Aire	1 10	1 4
Lerwick to Dunrossness	2 10	2
Cunningsburgh to Sands Aire		3
Hosewick to Levenwick		2

On the West Side

	A 6 oar boat. Scots.	A 4 oar boat. Scots.
From Spigga to Houss	1 10	1 4
Houss to Scallaway, ...	10	6
Bigtown to Houss	1 4	18
Mawick to Houss	10	6
Quarf to Scallaway	10	6
Scallaway to Ustaness	10	6
Scallaway to Sand or Rewick	18	12
Scallaway to Bixseter	1 4	18
Scallaway to Vallay	2	1 10
Sailavoe, or Gruten to Valay	15	10
Valay to Papastour, ...	1 4	18
Papa Sound	8	6
Papa to Eshaness or Helwick	1 4	18
Papa to Nounsburgh, or Seater, ...	18	12
Papa to Busta	1 16	1 4
Busta to Hilswick, and from Hilswick to Marruend	1 4	18

From

	A 6 oar boat. Scots.	A 4 oar boat. Scots.
From Hilswick to Hamer, 4 shillings, to Gunester, 6 p.		
Busta to Olnafirth, Gonfirth, or Papa Little	10	6
Busta to Aith, or Brinasiter	18	12
Busta to Sandness	1 10	1 4

The land fares in Zetland is, for horse-hire, one shilling Scots, the mile, and something to the boy ; for a post with a letter one shilling, said money, per mile out, or for carrying any light burden the same.

NUMBER VI.

Country Act anent Parochial Schools.

AT Lerwick, the 14th of November, 1724, anent proposals for erecting parochial schools in Zetland, in presence of Thomas Gifford of Busta, stuart and justiciar depute of Zetland, sitting in judgment, the whole heritors in Zetland present by themselves or their proxies, of which proposals the tenor follows in these words : Proposals unto the Gentlemen heritors of Zetland, anent settling parochial schools there, as law provides. As it is not unknown to any of you, that there is no legal school settled in any parish of this country, so there is none can pretend ignorance of the laws and acts of parliament made thereanent, whereby it is ordered and strictly observed throughout the whole kingdom of Scotland, that a legal school be erected in each parish thereof, as particularly by act W. par. I. ses. 6th. cha. 26. ratifying all former acts anent schools and schoolmasters, by which act the heritors of each parish are obliged to settle a fund for maintaining a school not under 100 marks Scots money yearly, nor exceeding 200 marks said money : and although that good and necessary law has not yet obtained in this country, yet certainly we are no less bound to the observation thereof than any other place within the said kingdom, nor can the same be supposed less necessary here than any where else ; nay, it is plainly obvious to any thinking person, that the gross ignorance and immorality that doth every where abound here, is chiefly if not solely, owing to the want of that early education and instruction of children, not only in the knowledge of letters, but also in the principles of our holy religion, which a school in each parish would in a great measure supply ; and to insist upon the usefulness and necessity of such parochial schools were superfluous, seeing it is not presumable that any good man will either dispute that, or refuse to contribute his utmost reasonable endeavours to propagate a work so pious and beneficial to the country, for in whatever parish a

6   legal

legal school is once settled, beside the benefit of that school; if the parish is discontiguous so as one school cannot serve the whole parish, they are, upon a right representation thereof, intitled to a school from the Society for Propagating of Christian Knowledge, whereas the parish where no legal school is settled has no title thereunto.   Now the grand objection against erecting these legal schools in this country is, that the heritage, or land rent, in most parishes here, is so inconsiderable, that the small heritors are not able to support the charge thereof; for obviating of which difficulty, although it cannot be denied but the charge thereof will be a greater burden upon the small heritors of Zetland, than upon most places in Scotland, yet considering the great benefit that may thereby arise to the poor inhabitants, it can be demonstrate if the heritors are willing and unanimous, there is not a parish in Zetland but can afford one hundred marks yearly, without any great burden upon the heritors, according to this method, that seeing there is no certain valuation of land-rent here, let that fund for the school be laid on in the same manner the cess is upon the marks of land, and the tenants to be the first advancers thereof, and the one half of what they advance to be allowed them out of the land rent; and thus there are some parishes in Zetland that by an imposition of one shilling Scots upon the markland will amount to upwards of one hundred pounds Scots: other parts there are that are at the rate of one shilling and sixpence, said money will surely amount to 100 marks, so that it can be left to the discretion of the heritors in each parish to proportion it upon the land as they shall see cause, the quota not being under 100 marks yearly; and this being agreeable to the method proposed in the act of parliament, and common practice throughout the kingdom, it is expected it will take the better in this place, or if any better method can be offered by any person or persons for effectuating of this pious and necessary design, let the same be produced to be considered of by all the gentlemen concerned, or any other needful amendments, and the fund being once settled, the direction thereof to be left to the heritors, minister, and kirk session in each parish, to be improven to the best advantage for promoting the end thereby designed.   T. G.

Lerwick, November 13th, 1724, the above proposals were read in open court, the whole heritors present, who took the same to adviseand on till to-morrow at ten of the clock in the forenoon, being the 14th day of the said month: the said day the heritors under subscribing having deliberately considered the above proposals, did unanimously go in thereunto, upon the conditions and under the restrictions following; viz. ' that the fund above proposed be levied out of those lands commonly called King's Land, as well as the Udell land, by an equal proportion upon the marks of land; and, 2dly, that the said fund should be under the direction of the heritors; and also the nomination of the schoolmaster,

and

and scat of the school in the respective parishes, shall be, with the special advice and consent of the heritors ; and in case of any schoolmaster being placed in any parish without consent foresaid, the heritors to be liberate from the payment of the fund above proposed ; the heritors also having power to present a fit person for collecting of the said fund as proportioned upon the land by them in each parish ; and in testimony whereof they did subscribe the same with their hands, and craved an act of court thereupon ; and that extracts thereof should be transmitted to the several baillies and principal heritors in each ministrie ; subscribed by Robert Sinclair, Laurence Bruce, James Mitchell, William Dick, Magnus Henderson, Andrew Scott, George Pitcarne, Robert Cragie, Robert Bruce, William Bruce, Thomas Hendrie, Robert Sinclair, John Laurence Stuart, Hector Scott, James Dunbar.

The Judge having seen and considered the premises, and finding the gentlemen heritors above-mentioned had unanimously gone into the proposals and method above laid down, for raising an annual fund in each parish in Zetland, for the maintenance of a school under the restrictions foresaid ; and that the said fund may be made effectual in manner and for the end above proposed, did interpose, and hereby interpose the authority of the Stuart Court of Zetland thereto, and ordains the same to be recorded in the books thereof, and extracts of the same to be transmitted to the baillies and principal heritors of each parish ; and in regard the right honourable the earl of Morton's concurrence thereto is not yet obtained, that his lordship's tenants may not be distressed for payment of the said fund until his consent be procured ; and that for each extract, the clerk extractor be paid a crown. (Signed) T. G. extracted J. G.

[DR. ARTHUR EDMONSTON, in his " VIEW of the Ancient and Modern State of the ZETLAND ISLANDS," 2 vols. 8vo, 1809, re-marks, that " the peasantry of Zetland are not more illiterate than the same class of society in the northern parts of Scotland. They are naturally sagacious, and anxious to improve themselves. Un-till lately there were but few parish schools in the country, but they are now introduced into every parish, and scholars of both sexes attend with a degree of zeal that does them the highest credit. Besides being able to teach them to read and write, most of the schoolmasters understand arithmetic, and a few are ac-quainted even with the elementary parts of navigation." As re-spects the " Proposals for erecting Parochial Schools in Zetland," he goes on to say, " I have stated the limited sources of instruc-tion to which, until lately, the poorer classes of society in Zetland had access, and the advantages likely to result from the more general diffusion of intelligence. The ancestors of the present proprietors of land, were early impressed with a conviction of the truth of this observation, and this SPIRITED, SENSIBLE, AND PATRIOTIC RESOLUTION DOES THEM THE HIGHEST CREDIT."]

NUMBER

NUMBER VI1.

A Compend of the Country Acts for directing the Rancell-
    Men, and Society for regulating of Servants, and
    Reformation of Manners, with their Instructions.

AT Burravoe, the 17th day of November 1725, a circuit court
holden by Thomas Gifford, of Busta, stuart and justiciar depute
of Zetland, there were several petitions from some of the kirk
sessions and heritors of Zetland presented· and read in open court,
containing in substance the following words :—

That amongst many, the gross sins and immoralites which
abound in Zetland, that of servants, unfaithfulness, negligence,
and disobedience to their masters, is none of the least common,
together with sabbath-breaking, cursing, swearing, ignorance, irre-
ligion, stealing, lying, adultery, fornication, malice, envy, covet-
ousness, drunkenness, disobedience to parents, and that abominable fewds betwixt husband and wife, turning even to sinful
separation with some, &c. are the just deserving causes why a holy
and sin-revenging God is justly provoked to inflict judgments upon
this place, if a speedy repentance and reformation be not set about
by all persons in their respective stations and capacities ; and for
the better effectuating such necessary reformation, it may not be
impertinent to condescend upon some of the most obvious causes of
these abounding abominations to be considered of, and as far prevented for the future as possible. As first, ignorance of God, and
the principles of our holy religion, which leadeth many into a
contempt of and slighting the gospel and ordinances thereof. 2nd,
Fulness of bread and plenty, which the Lord hath been pleased
to continue for some time, sadly and sinfully abused by the gene-
rality of the ingratefull receivers thereof. 3d, Negligence and
slackness in the magistrate, the minister, the elder, the rancelman,
and masters of families, in the zealous, prudent, and conscientious
performance of their respective duties. 4th, Criminal neglect of
parents in the education of their children ; not a few such unna-
tural parents there are, who do not only slight the opportunity
good providence hath laid to their hand of having their children
at least taught to read the holy scriptures, but also are at no pains
to have them trained up in the knowledge of our holy religion,
nor to acquaint them with that honest labour and industry which
might put them in a capacity to earn their bread, when grown up,
and make them useful in the place where they live, it being
rather the practice of many graceless parents by their evil example
to poison their children with many vicious habits, or at least to
bring them up in sloth and ignorance, allowing them to do what
they please, and thereby not only ruining their children, but
also bringing themselves under the guilt of perjury. 5th, The
frequent marriages of such as have no visible stock whereupon to
                                                                subsist,

subsist, many young fellows having no sooner got whole cloaths, but they imagine themselves too genteel to serve, and being once married and set up for themselves, they can live as they list ; and thus many such are quickly reduced, either to extreme poverty, or tempted to bad practices, whereby also a generation of idle beggars is produced, and the families of honest and industrious people are reduced and brought low for want of servants. These, and such like, being the causes of many calamities already felt, and more yet feared by us ; we most humbly beg the civil magistrate to take the same under his most serious consideration, and not only to cause the good laws against profaneness and immorality to be put to vigorous executions, but also to make acts agreeable thereunto and adapted to the peculiar circumstances of this country, for suppressing of sin and immorality, and promoting of piety and virtue, by inflicting of condign punishment upon all wilful transgressors of God's holy law, and thereby proving indeed a terror to evil doers, and for a praise to these that do well.

The said stuart depute, having considered the foresaid petitions and representations, and finding the desire thereto both reasonable and necessary, is willing to do what in his power for putting the laws to due execution, conform to the will and tenor thereof, as far as is competent to him upon any just and regular application made to him for that end. But it appears evident, that the cause why transgressors of the law, and disturbers of the peace pass with impunity is because elders, rancelmen, and masters of families, are negligent in their duty, as having the first inspection of and daily access to know the lives and manners of all persons in their families and respective bounds, some of them being ignorant of the danger they incur by such neglect, and others coniveing at the faults of those they are either unwilling or afraid to reprove, or inform against, foolishly imagining it safer to sin against God by their silence than to offend their fellow-creature, and therefore do not only involve themselves in the guilt of other people's sins, but also become guilty of that heinous sin of perjury in acting perfidiously in the duties of their station and office ; for which cause, and that such irregularities may be prevented as far as possible for the future, it appears absolutely necessary that elders and rancelmen should be strictly enjoined by the respective judicatories of whom they hold their office, that they carefully and diligently perform the duties incumbent on them, conform to the solemn oaths they have come under so to do, and that under the pain of being prosecuted as perjured persons, and punished accordingly ; and for making the laws as intelligible as possible, unto all persons so far as relates to the more obvious immoralities that prevail in this place, the following acts and directions are entered by authority of the said stuart court, and ordained to be observed as founded upon and agreeable to the laws of this kingdom, and the old country acts.

Act

Act 1. That no person or persons within the country of Zetland travel by sea or land upon a sabbath day about any secular affairs, nor use any work, business, or recreation, lawful on other days, save in works of necessity and mercy, under the pain of four pounds Scots for the first fault, and eight pounds said money for the second, besides satisfying the kirk for the scandal; and those that cannot pay to be punished in their persons, and if thereafter found guilty, to be proceeded against as the law directs, with the utmost rigour; and that each person wilfully sitting at home from the kirk on the Lord's-day, or withdrawing from divine service, who can give no good reason for their so doing, shall pay for each time twenty shillings Scots, and such as cannot pay to be punished in their persons; one-third of these fines to belong to the informer or prosecutor, and two-thirds to the poor.

2. That all persons within the parish punctually attend upon diets of catechising, and family visitation as appointed by the minister, under the pain of twenty shillings said money, to be paid by each person absent if they can give no reasonable cause for their absence, the master or mistress of the family being liable *primo instante* for all persons in the family, having recourse against the offenders; one-third of the fines to the prosecutor, and two-thirds to the poor.

3. That each profane curser, swearer, or liar, shall pay for each fault twenty shillings said money; and if habitually found so, to be also punished in their persons; one-third of the fines to the informer, and two-thirds to the poor.

4. That any person being found to drink drunk shall for the first fault pay half a crown, for the second a crown, and if found habitually so, to be punished in their persons, and fined as law directs; and whosoever giveth, or selleth drink to such habitual drinkers, shall also be liable to the foresaid fines and punishments.

5. That no person scold with, nor provoke their neighbour, nor any other person by abusive language, under the pain of three pounds said money, for the first fault; and if found to be habitual scolds and disturbers of the peace, to be punished in their persons, and fined at the discretion of the judge, and as provided by law.

6. That each parent who wilfully neglects to put their children to school, when conveniently they can do it, and does not teach them to read, shall pay yearly double the tax due by him of the Fund for maintaining the parochial school, and also a fine of three pounds said money for the use of the poor scholars.

7. That every master of a family have all his children and servants instructed in the principles of our holy religion, and taught the shorter catechism, at least use his utmost endeavour for that end, under the pain of three pounds said money, to be paid by such who are found negligent in that duty, for the use of the poor; and that masters impose nothing upon their servants that is either unlawful or unreasonable, nor with-hold from them

what

what is their due, either in meat or fee, conform to agreement, and the country practice, under the pain of three pounds said money.

8. That whatsoever servant, male or female, shall wilfully disobey their master or mistress's lawful commands, or give them provoking and unbecoming language, shall in the first place be liable to rebuke, exhortation, and moderate correction; and if they notwithstanding continue to offend, shall, upon the first complaint against them being proven, lose half a year's fee, and also be punished in their persons as their offence shall be found to deserve; and that no servant remove from their service, but upon lawful warning of their master or mistress half a year before the term they design to remove, and that before a rancleman, or one of the members of society for regulating of servants, who are to witness such warning whenever required thereunto; and that upon reasonable grounds to be judged of by the said society, or any three of them, and that none otherways remove, unless it be with the mutual consent of master and servant, under the pain of half a year's fee, besides personal punishment; and that no person receive nor entertain in their houses any servant who shall have contrary to this act gone away from their masters, under the pain of half a mark, Scots money, for each night they keep such servant, after being advertised thereof; and that no master or mistress thrust out their servant without due warning as above; and in case of a servant becoming invalid through sickness, old age, or accident, that they care for, and maintain them untill application be made for having such invalid settled upon the public charge of the parish, as is usual in such case, and the same obtained, under the pain of three pounds said money, besides damages to the servant so thrust out, as the baillie shall see reasonable.

9. That none practise upon, or intice another man's servant; nor fee a servant, but at the sight and in the presence of a rancelman, or one of the members of the society, who can vouch the servant's being free to fee, under the pain of three pounds Scots, to be paid by the inticer or feer, and forty shillings said money by the feed, besides losing the servant.

10. That none keep more servants or working people in their families than what they have absolute occasion for, while others want servants; but that the society for regulating of servants appoint them to part with such as they see needful, for supply of such as want, under the pain of half a mark for each night they keep the servant appointed, besides damages to the person to whom they are appointed.

11. That in such families where they have no servants but their own children, that some of those children be appointed to other service, and if need be, appoint them a servant in place of the child or children removed, so as there may be at least one servant in the family, besides the children, under the pain of half a mark each night the person appointed is kept back.

12.

12. That none entertain in their families idle persons that are capable to work, nor such as are called house-folk ; but that the said society appoint them to service, under the pain of half a mark for each night, to be paid by the person who keeps them after such appointment.

13. That none keep scar sheep, save in holms, under the pain of ten pounds.

14. That none conceal their tythes of any sort, under the pain of ten pounds Scots money.

15. That none keep unjust weights and measures to buy and sell upon, under the pain of ten pounds said money.

16. That all the poor people incapable to work for their bread, and having no children capable to maintain them, be quartered in the parish for maintenance, and that they have money out of the poor's box for buying of clothes, and that none of them be allowed to go out of the respective quarters to which they are appointed ; and when they die, that they have a chist and winding sheet, out of the poor's box, and that no householder refuse to receive the poor appointed to him in his turn, under the pain of forty shillings, said money.

17. That none be allowed to marry, who has not forty pounds Scots of free gear to set up house upon, or some lawful trade whereby to subsist, nor such as cannot read, and is someway capable to demean himself as a Christian master of a family ; and that the foresaid society inquire thereunto, and suffer none otherways to marry.

18. That no master of a family entertain in his service any servant belonging to another parish three months, without a testimonial from the parish where he was born, under the pain of three pounds, said money, and losing the servant ; and that no servant remove from one parish to serve in another, until first making application to the society for regulating of servants, who not finding such servant as good encouragement as they can have elsewhere, then they are to recommend them to the session for a testimonial, and then they are free to serve in any parish they please, providing such servant bring securities from the baillie or kirk session of the parish where they are to settle, that in case they shall through old age, sickness, or accident, be rendered incapable to serve, that they shall be maintained at the charge of that parish ; and not to be returned back to the parish where they were born when unable to do any thing for themselves, as has been the common practice ; and if no such security be given, that such servant be charged to return to the parish where they were born within three months after their departure, under the pain of ten pounds Scots, to be paid by the master of such servant, and six pounds, said money, by the servant, besides personal punishment in case of refusal.

19. That the society for regulating of servants appoint them
reasonable

reasonable fees according as they deserve, and is common in the country ; and that no servant be compelled to serve any master who does not give them meat and fee duly and seasonably, conform to agreement.

20. That no persons within the parish, on the sabbath-day, bring their horses within the dicks of the kirk town, nor teather them there, without liberty granted by the proprietor, or tenant, under the pain of forty shillings Scots, for each time.

21. That no person within the parish sell old corn over year, and refuse to assist his neighbours in labouring time with seed and fodder, they paying him the highest price therefore that goes in the country, under the pains of ten pounds.

22. That no person bring any butter for payment of land-rent, or otherways to be sold, but such as is clean from hairs, bland, and other dirt, and sufficiently salted, under the pain of forty shillings Scots, for each insufficient parcel presented ; and for the first fault, the insufficient butter to be returned to the owner ; and for the second, the butter to be forfault for the use of the poor of the parish.

23. That no persons present fish-oil for payment of any rent, or for sale, but such as is sufficiently boiled thin, free of drag, and all other mixture, under the pain of forty shillings for each insufficient parcel thereof presented ; and that lawrightmen be appointed for receiving the butter and oil, conform to the old country act.

24. That all coarse stockings for sale be made of double yarn sufficiently walked, under the pains contained in the acts there anent made.

25. For encouragement of fishing, upon which the general benefit of the country very much depends, that every householder who is not a fisher, and having servants or sons capable to go to sea, be allowed to go with any fisher that wants them, for reasonable fees, the months of May, June, and July, the one-half of which fee so earned to belong to the master, and the other half to the servant, beside his whole ordinary fee ; and that the society for regulating of servants appoint reasonable fees for all servants both for land and sea service, so as masters may not be imposed upon, nor servants defrauded of what is their due ; and that both masters and servants observe the said appointment, under the pain of three pounds Scots money.

26. Anent making of rancelmen, and their instructions.

In a baillie court, lawfully fenied, the whole householders in the parish being present, the baillie is to cause his clerk to read out a list of such honest men in the parish as are fit to be rancelmen, and then he is to enquire each of them, if they are willing to accept of the office of rancelman, and if any of them refuse, and can give no good reason for his refusal to accept, the baillie may fine him in ten pounds Scots ; and those that accept, the baillie is to

enquire

enquire of the whole householders present, if they have ought to object against either of these men, why they may not be made rancelmen, and no objection being made, then the following instructions are to be read to them :—

I. You are at any time, night or day you see needfull, to call for assistance, and to enter within any house within the parish, and search the same as narrowly as you can ; and upon any suspicion of theft, if they refuse you keys, you are to break open their doors or chests, and if you find anything that is stolen, you are to bring the thief and the fang to the baillie, or secure both, and acquaint the baillie ; if you have any scruple about any thing you find in the house, you are to enquire how they came by it, and if they refuse to tell, take witness upon their refusal, and let the thing be secured till you acquaint the baillie ; you are also to examine the house-stores of flesh and meale, and see if they be correspondent to their stocks, and likewise the wool, yarn, webs, stockings, &c. and enquire how they came by all these, and if they cannot give a satisfactory account thereof, and brough and hamele, you are to inform against them.

II. You are to enquire into the lives and conversations of families, whether there is any discord or unbecoming carriage betwixt husband and wife, parent and child, master and servant, or any other unchristian or unlawful practice in the family : you are to rebuke such and exhort them to amend ; and if they obey it is well ; if not, you are faithfully to represent such to the judicatory competent, and bring the best evidence you can against all such offenders.

III. You are to prevent all quarrels and scoldings as far as in your power, by commanding the contending parties to the peace, and if they persist, require witness against them, and call for assistence to separate them, and give in a faithfnl report thereof to the fiscal, or clerk of court ; and in case you are not witness to any scolding or quarrelling that happens, you are to gather the best information thereof you can, and make report of the same as aforesaid.

IV. If you hear any person cursing or swearing, you are to demand of them the fine ; and if they refuse to pay it, you are to require witness against and report it to the court, one-third of which fine is to yourself, and two-thirds to the poor.

V. That you narrowly enquire in your neighbourhood who sits at home from the kirk on the sabbath-day, and from diets of catechising ; and if they can give no sufficient reason for their so doing, that you cause them to pay the fine, to be applied as aforesaid ; and that you take particular notice in your neighbourhood anent keeping the sabbath-day, and if you find any breach thereof, that you report the same.

VI. You are strictly to observe the country acts anent keeping good neighbourhood, such as that none injure others in their grass and

and corn, and rebuke the offenders, with certification if they continue so to do you will inform the court against them; and that they build their dicks sufficiently and timeously under the pains contained in the act.

VII. That tenants do not abuse their lands nor demolish their houses through sloth and carelessness; that you reprove such, and if they continue so to do, acquaint the land master.

VIII. You are to enquire if there is in your neighbourhood any idle vagrant person, and to acquaint such, that they must either betake themselves to some honest employment, or you will inform against them, so as they may be punished and ordered to service; and that the poor be taken care of in their respective quarters, and not suffered to stray abroad; nor are you to allow any beggar or thigger from any other parish to pass through your bounds; and, if they offer so to do, you will secure them till they be punished, conform to the country act.

IX. That you try all the dogs in your quarter, and that none be allowed to keep a dog that can take a sheep, unless he is allowed to keep a sheep-dog by the baillie; and that none keep scar sheep otherways nor in the act, and that the acts be observed anent punding, hounding, marking and taking of sheep.

X. You are to enquire in your quarter anent all persons using any manner of witchcraft, charms, or any other abominable and devilish superstitions, and faithfully inform against such so as they may be brought to condign punishment.

XI. You are to examine all tradesmen in your bounds, and see that they make sufficient work, and do not impose upon any in their prices; and if you find any such transgressors, that you inform against them, so as they may be punished as the law directs.

XII. Upon any suspicion of theft, two or three rancelmen may take as many witnesses with them, and go to the neighbour parish and rancell, and if they catch a thief, they are to acquaint the Baillie of that parish thereof, who will order the thief to be secured.

And in the last place, as you are intrusted with a power of inspecting the lives and manners of others, so let your own good life and conversation be exemplary unto them for good, and take care you are not found guilty of those faults yourselves, that you are called to reprove in others, for if ye should, your punishment shall be double to theirs; now all these instructions, as far as it is in your power, you promise and swear solemnly in the sight of Almighty God, and as you shall answer to him at the great day, faithfully and honestly to observe and perform.

Act. 27. That no person in any way impede, maltreat, or abuse a rancelman in the full and free exercise of his office, under the pain of ten pounds Scots money, beside personal punishment, and a greater fine as the offence given shall be found to deserve; and that none refuse to aid and assist a rancelman in the execution of

his

his office when required thereunto, under the like pain of ten pounds money foresaid.

NUMBER VIII.

Commission and Instructions to the Society for regulating of Servants and Reformation of Manners.

IN a bailie court, the whole house-holders in the parish being present, a list of the most intelligent honest men in the parish whom the baillie designs to erect into a society, being read, and they answering to their names, the following instructions being read to them ; the baillie inquires at each of them, if they are willing to accept of and enter into that society, which if they accept, then the baillie asketh the whole house-holders present, if they have ought to object against either of these men, why they should not be admitted as members of that society ; and if no objection is offered, and they being all formerly elders, or raucelmen, they are judicially sworn and admitted :

1. You are as often as you see cause, in a civil and discreet manner to inspect all families within the parish, and at least twice in the year, and to enquire how masters discharge the duties incumbent upon them towards their children and servants ; if children are obedient to their parents, and if servants are honest, obedient, and tractable to their masters ; and if either are deficient, you are to exhort them to amend under the pains contained in the act there anent : and if thereafter they persist in any irregularity, that you inform against them, so that they may be punished accordingly.

2. You are to enquire what working people are in the family, and conform to the necessary work they have to do, and the necessity of others ; and you are at any time to appoint such servants as can be spared, out of one to go to another family that hath absolute need of them ; and the officer having charged the servant to remove according to your appointment, under pain of half a mark to be paid by the master, or any persons, each night the servant is thereafter kept, which you have power to strass them for ; also for the fines of cursers, swearers, and wilfull absenters from the kirk and catechising, conform to the act, one half of which fines go to yourselves, and the other half to the poor ; as and that you allow no idle person to stay in any family that is capable to work ; and that you appoint all servants such reasonable fees as they shall deserve, and see them duly paid thereof, conform to the act.

3. That you hear all complaints betwixt masters and servants, and determine betwixt them, conform to justice ; and that you
allow

allow no servant to enter to or remove from service otherways than according to the act there anent.

4. That any three of your number is a quorum in determining in any matter relating to servants, conform to the acts there anent; and if any difficulty appear you are to consult the baillie.

5. That you see the acts observed in your bounds, anent putting of children to school, and anent keeping the sabbath-day.

6. You endeavour to supply fishers with men, conform to the act thereanent, so as no honest man's boat be set ashore for want of men, and that you appoint reasonable fees or hire for those that serve at sea, and see them duly paid; and that if masters maltreat their servants, that you order such servant to those who will use them better.

7. That the whole society meet twice in the year; and any member wilfully absent from that meeting, to be fined in twenty shillings Scots; at which general meetings you are to common upon all the irregularities in the parish, and of what has been done by each of you in his bounds for preventing of immorality, and promoting virtue, and of what may be further necessary for that end; and that your instructions, and the acts you are to be ruled by anent servants, be read in your meetings; and if any of your number shall be found deficient in his duty, you are to admonish him to amend, under the pain of being informed against and turned off with disgrace; and that you endeavour to suppress all vice and immorality, and encourage virtue and piety to the utmost of your power, conform to the acts there anent made, which is your rule; and that you choose your own process at each general meeting; and that all disputes be carried by plurality of suffrages, or most votes.

And, lastly, seeing you are invested with a power to rule over and inspect the lives and manners of others, it will be your credit, as well as your duty, to shew yourselves patrons of piety and virtue; and in case you are found guilty of those faults you are set to reprove in others, you may expect that your punishment will be double to theirs; upon these conditions you enter into their society, and judicially promise in the presence of God Almighty, that you will do your utmost for advancing the glory of God, the public peace, and welfare of the place where you live, as far as you are capable, conform to the above instructions, as your subscription hereof doth witness. The whole foresaid acts and instructions being published in open court, the judge ordains the authority of the stuart and justiciar court to be interponed thereto; and that the same be recorded in the stuart court books of Zetland, and extracts thereof to be given out by the clerk to the baillies desiring the same, upon payment of the clerks dues. Signed T. G.

NUMBER

NUMBER IX.

A Scheme anent regulating the German and Danish current money passing here.

That forasmuch as German and Danish current money hath for many years by gone passed in Zetland, stoyvers for pence sterling, without any regard to the intrinsick value, or any authority from the government for their so doing; but on the contrary, all foreign money is ordained by act of parliament to pass only as bullion, according to the weight and finesse thereof, of which it is not to be supposed many here are competent judges, and therefore these foreign species has continued to pass with us under the denominations they bear in the places where they are made, and at the rate of pence for stoyvers, which currency having once obtained, encouraged many to import that specie, rather than any other, which they must have purchased at a dearer rate, so that now there is scarce any other money to be seen in the country, and although the importation of that kind of money might be beneficial to some particular persons, such as all traders upon Hamburgh, yet it has been very prejudicial to the country in general in several respects, as first the real value of these foreign species being unknown, all goods sold therefore, or bought therewith, was still at an uncertain compute, so that money which serves in every country, as the only rule to ascertain the value of all things that are bought and sold, has been of no such use to us since that unknown specie proved the standard, and passed far above his intrinsick value.

2. It is no small disadvantage to the country to have that money in return for its product exported, which cannot pass in any part of Great Britain and so cannot therewith pay the land-tax, crown-rent, customs, and excise, nor can they therewith buy victuals, and other things absolutely necessary, which brings many under a necessity to exchange that foreign money at considerable discount.

3. That notwithstanding that foreign money hath long passed here in buying and selling, and is the most, if not only specie to be seen, yet there is none obliged by law to take it in payment of any sum due by bonds, bills, and others, payable in British money, but as bullion, or any other merchandise, at the pleasure of the buyer, which has proven a hardship upon many, and in the last place, to add no more, those German and Danish current money passeth no where in Europe, save only in the respective places where they are coined, and even there at the greatest uncertainty; and still far below that, which they call their bank money; as for instance, they have of late called down at Hamburgh their 6 stiver pieces to 5 stivers, and their other species proportionably; so that for Zetland to keep up a constant overvalue upon that

money

money which is so despicable and precarious every where else, were to act a part no less unreasonable, than hurtful and pernicious to itself; for which cause, and as far as possible to prevent these inconveniences for the future, it appears absolutely necessary either to discharge the said foreign species to pass at all otherways than as bullion, as the law directs, or that the sum be brought to a par with our sterling money; but taking the last as the most eligible, because the real value of these foreign species cannot be known on account of their various species and no less variety of metals in the composition whereof they consist, so that a trial of that nature as it would be very difficult, so it might prove hurtful to many, but allowing that foreign money to be computed according to the current course of exchange, and that estimate put upon them in those countries where they are coined, which certainly must be their full value, why then just now at Hamburgh 18 mark lubts goes to one pound sterling, which makes the difference betwixt stivers and pence 20 per cent., and even that computation is 5 per cent. less than the common difference betwix their current and bank-money, however the foresaid compute of twenty pounds per cent. discount will serve to bring the said foreign species as near to a par with sterling money as is necessary to make it pass at no higher value with us than it does at Hamburgh, from whence only it is imported here; and that we should keep up their current money so far undervalued by themselves upon a level with our sterling-money is both unreasonable and unlawful, and therefore the said German and Danish current money ought and should, with the unanimous consent of the country, be ordained to pass at the aforesaid discount of 20 per cent. and for making which discount more intelligible, one stiver is ⅛ of a penny sterling, or ten pennies Scots, six stoyvers is five shillings Scots, and twenty-four stoyvers is one pound Scots, and all other foreign coin to pass here as it doth in any other part of Britain, and seeing the above proposed regulation is founded upon reason, and the statute laws of Great Britain, it is not doubted but this whole country will readily go in thereunto, without any further publick intimation thereof, or authority interponed thereto, to enforce the observance of the same, but the obvious interest of the country in general, and as the same is agreeable to the acts of parliament in that behalf made; but that the whole country may act in concert in that matter, and that the benefit of loss thereby may be equal to all according to their respective concern therein, appoints the stewart clark to transmit a copy hereof to each baillie within the country to be intimate to all persons within their baulleries, to be by them observed as far as the same is agreeable to the laws of the nation, the good of the country, and the common dictates of reason; and if there is any just objections there against or any needful amendments to be put thereto, let the same be brought to the next head-court, to be considered of as accords.   T. G.

NUMBER

NUMBER X.

Two LETTERS from Captain THOMAS PRESTON to JOSEPH
AMES, F.R.S. [Author of the " Typographical Antiquities of Great Britain and Ireland," 4to, 1749, &c.]

DEAR SIR,   Zetland, Jan. 31, 1743-4.

YOUR favour of the 2d of June came lately to hand.
Nothing but a sight of you could equal the pleasure it brought
me, with an account of your welfare.   I wrote to you ten months
since, with some letters to other friends, but these all miscarried ;
the opportunity by which I send this is very unexpected, for this
island has very rarely any correspondence with the rest of the
world for the six winter months ; for the year may be said to
contain ten months of winter, and two of cold, raw weather.   I
thought it very absurd to hear the inhabitants complain of heat,
at the same instant I complained of cold, and wished for a great
coat.   They are so accustomed to stormy bad weather, that they
will venture to sea in small boats when you would not venture to
cross the Thames.   I shall give you a short description of this
Island.

It is the northmost belonging to Scotland, set between the
latitudes of 60 and 61 degrees ; its length is N. and S. 60 miles,
its breadth 30, and so divided into headlands, and smaller islands,
rocks, bays, inlets, and coves, &c. that you cannot place a com-
pass in any the most inland part of its chart that shall be two
miles from the sea, which makes it extremely difficult to make a
good chart of the island, of which there is no chart extant worth
naming.   During my long stay, I have devoted some of my
(otherwise) idle time in making observations and surveying the
place, by which, and suitable information gained from the inhabitants, I have a sea chart, which I flatter myself may be of
great use to other navigators, who are all strangers to the many
safe and good harbours in this island, and several capable of receiving many large ships.   The land is wild, barren, and mountainous, nor is there so much as a tree or bush to be seen.   The
shores are difficult, and in many places inaccessible, rude, steep,
and iron like, the sight of which strikes the mind with a certain
dread and horror, and such monstrous precipices, and hideous
rocks, as bring all Brobdingnag before your thoughts.   I doubt
not but you are now listening out for some account of curiosities of art and nature, which most here are strangers to, and yet
this island is not quite barren of ; but not having room here, must
defer an account thereof till it pleases God I see you.

In winter the sun sets soon after it rises, and in summer it
rises soon after setting ; so that the night at that season is near as
light as the day, and the day in December is near as dark as the
night in the winter sets here.

We

We see every night the Aurora Borealis, I think you call it, but we seamen the Northern Lights, which spreads a broad glaring light over the whole hemisphere, and looks somewhat terrifying to them not used to it.

I shall only mention (lest I tire your patience) that a comet has appeared to us for some time from the West, large and plain to the naked eye.

Yours,

THOMAS PRESTON.

Captain THOMAS PRESTON to Mr. AMES.

DEAR SIR, Leith, May 12, 1744.

THIS informs you of my safe arrival at this place, where I met your kind letter of no date. I have seen Mr. Ruddiman, who says, you shall hear from him in a few days, but cannot give you much encouragement as to subscription. He promises to give you what assistance he can as to the book itself.

In my last from Zetland, I gave you a short account of that country. I shall now give you some more particulars under that head, just as they occur to my memory. The island is called by the Dutch *Hetland*, by us commonly *Shetland;* but the proper name of it is *Zetland*. Within there are 30 parish churches, and 80 gentlemen's houses, besides the towns *Lervic* and *Scalleway*. It was first inhabited by the *Pihts* or *Picts*, who were driven out by the *Danes*. Christian king of Denmark and Norway, whose daughter, the lady Margaret, was given in marriage to king James III. of Scotland in the year 1463, agreed that the island of Orkney and Zetland should be in the possession of the said king James till he had paid him 50000 florins of the Rhine for his daughter's dowry; and Christian afterwards on the birth of a young prince, his grandson, called James, renounced his title to the said islands in favour of king James, and they have ever since belonged to Scotland. Zetland lies between the latitude 60 and 61 degrees, the longest distant but little from the east part of Scotland. The longest day is near 20 hours. I have read a very small print in my chamber at midnight with the windows shut. The air is temperate, considering the country lies so far north, and agrees tolerable well with them that can endure cold and a thick fog. I must own I have not found the winters so cold as in other parts of Great Britain; nor are the summers near so warm, for which indeed the length of the days make some amends. I have heard that some fishermen have affirmed that at sea they are near the sun's body at midnight; but that is impossible, since the sun

7 on

on the shortest day in December is four hours above the horison, and it must certainly be deprest as long under it in June. The winters are more subject to rain than snow. Nor does frost and snow continue so long on the ground as on the mainland of Great Britain; yet I have seen the ground wholly covered with snow the second of May last year. The winds during the long winter season continue to blow most boisterously generally between the S. and W. which occasion many shipwrecks. There have been three or four on the island in my time. The land is mountainous and moorish, abounding with moss and heather, under which they dig peat or turf for firing; under that are hard rocks. Their horses are very little, but strong and well mettled, which they call *Shelties*. Their oxen, swine, and sheep, of which last they have plenty, and their cattle of all kinds, are small. The price of a horse is a guinea, an ox somewhat less, a sheep half a crown, a sheep [lamb ?] sixpence; rabbits they have in some parts of the country. Frogs and toads there are none, nor perhaps any poisonous vermin; there are many otters which they call *Tikes*, and seals which they call *Selkes;* sometimes there are many young whales, which they call *Pellack* or *Spout* whales. They run into creeks, and so entangle themselves among the rocks, that they are cast on the shore or easily taken. There is plenty of sea weeds, called *Tangle*, growing on rocks, of which may be made kelp for the making of soap. There is plenty of shell-fish of most kinds Their oysters are the best I ever ate. In the sea they catch cod, ling, haddock, whitings, scate, turbot, and herrings, colefish, flukes, trout, &c.

There are many sorts of wild fowl; namely, the dunter goose, clack goose, swans, ducks, teal, whaps, toists, liers, kittewacks, maws, plovers, scarfes, &c. There is likewise the ember goose, which is said to hatch her eggs under her wing. This is certain that none saw them on the land, or out of the water, and that they have a cavity, or hollow place under one of their wings, only capable of containing a large egg.

There are here very large eagles, which they call *Earns*, which prey upon the young lambs, &c. There is a law in force, that if any kill these eagles, he is to have a hen out of every house in the parish wherein it is killed, though it is never demanded.

I do not doubt but there are mines of silver, tin, and lead, in the country, for several sorts of minerals are to be found, and I have been credibly informed that pieces of pure massy silver of considerable bigness have been turned up by the plough; but such treasures are neglected, or not improved, through the poverty or carelessness of the proprietors. In many places marle quarries of excellent freestone, limestone, and slate, are found, and some veins of marble. Sometimes are cast up by the sea, timber, pieces of wreck, hogsheads of wine and brandy, and sometimes spermaceti, ambergreese, water-spunges, and cam-shells (*Os sepiæ*) are found on the shore,

There

There is no forest or wood, not so much as a tree, hardly a bush of any sort in the whole country, except in some gentlemen's gardens, and those never dare to peep over the garden-wall for fear of the north wind.

The country is so divided by the sea, that it cannot be expected there should be in it any rivers, yet there are many brooks and little runs of water called *bourns* and *lochs*, or lakes, many of which afford trouts, and I have eaten excellent cod fish that have been taken in one of these lochs or lakes of perfect fresh water, which have been very near the sea.

The people are generally civil, sagacious, of a ready wit, and of a quick apprehension, piously inclined, much given to hospitality, civil and liberal in their entertainments, and exceeding kind to strangers, which indeed I may say from experience, for I never met with more civility in any part of the world. They are generally of a dark complexion, personable and comely enough. The women are lovely, and the gentry go well drest, are genteel in carriage, well behaved in company, and smart and pleasant in conversation, even to a miracle, considering they live in such a remote island, which has so little correspondence with the rest of the world. They delight more in the conversation of men than in the tittle-tattle of their own sex. They are strangers to plays, operas, masquerades, assemblies, balls, set visiting days, extravagant dress, gallantry, &c. and are free from those innocent fashionable vices, which so much disgrace their betters. They are modest virgins, and virtuous wives ; for adultery is not known among them. Among the common sort fornication sometimes happens ; but their constancy is such, that they are sure to marry one among another ; nevertheless if a child happens to come in less than 9 months after marriage, they are both obliged by the law of Scotland, to do penance in church. This heinous sin the pious priests call ante-nuptial fornication. The name is of their own coining, and so is the sin too for aught I know, for I think it is somewhat odd that a man must suffer the censure of the kirk for going to bed to his own wife ; however if they find out new sins, they should invent new names.

The country is most commodious for navagation, which makes me wonder it has so long been neglected that we have not even so much as a map of it. There are more than 20 safe harbours of easy access capable of receiving large ships, the most remarkable of which are *Lerwick* or *Brassa Sound, Dura Voe*, and *Balta Sound*, on the West [East ?] side of the Country. The coast is all high and bold, and may be seen many leagues from the sea. There are no sands round the whole island, and but few sunken rocks, and those near the shore, except one dangerous shoal on the West side called *Have de Grind*, and some rocks on the N.W. above water, both which as well as the whole island, I have exactly surveyed, and I think without vanity I can say that I can produce a very

good

good map af Zetland, which I believe may be of great service, especially in war time.

I fear I have tired your patience with my long incoherent epistles; I shall therefore conclude with my kind love to all friends;

And am, dear SIR,

Your most affectionate humble Servant,

THOMAS PRESTON.

FINIS.

R. STME AND SON, PRINTERS, EDINBURGH.

LaVergne, TN USA
24 June 2010
187300LV00004B/60/P